QUILTER'S ACADEMY

Vol. 1—Freshman Year

A Skill-Building Course in Quiltmaking

Harriet Hargrave & Carrie Hargrave

C&T PUBLISHING

Text and photography copyright © 2009 by Harriet Hargrave and Carrie Hargrave

Illustrations copyright © 2009 by C&T Publishing, Inc.

Publisher: Amy Marson

Creative Director: Gailen Runge

Editor: Carrie Hargrave

Copyeditor/Proofreader: Wordfirm Inc.

Cover/Book Designer: Kristen Yenche

Production Coordinator: Casey Dukes

Illustrator: Aliza Shallit

Photography by Brian Birlauf

Cover photography by Christina Carty-Francis and Diane Pedersen of C&T Publishing, Inc.

Published by C&T Publishing, Inc., P.O. Box 1456, Lafayette, CA 94549

Library of Congress Cataloging-in-Publication Data
Hargrave, Harriet.
Quilter's Academy Vol 1.- Freshman Year : a skill-building course in quiltmaking / by Harriet Hargrave and Carrie Hargrave.
     p. cm.
ISBN 978-1-57120-594-0 (softcover)
1. Patchwork. 2. Quilting. I. Hargrave, Carrie, 1976- II. Title.
TT835.H3384 2009
746.46--dc22
2009008787

Printed in China

10 9 8 7 6 5 4 3

DEDICATION

We would like to dedicate this book to a very important woman who has influenced the world of quilting in untold ways, but whose name is unfamiliar to today's new quilters.

To Barbara Johannah, one of the earliest innovators of strip piecing and a passel of other fantastic ideas that we take for granted today—continuous-curve machine quilting, the use of mirrors for design, sheet method half-square triangles…the list goes on. Thank you for your inspiration and ideas.

We would also like to dedicate this book to all the thousands of Harriet's students who have influenced her desire to be the very best teacher she could be during the past 32 years. We hope the passion for quilting runs as deep in them as it does in us.

ACKNOWLEDGMENTS

A special thanks to everyone at C&T Publishing for giving us the opportunity to build a true study program through this series of books that brings us back to the very basics (and beyond) of great quiltmaking skills.

Sincere thanks to SewEzi for providing us with one of their wonderful portable tables and to Dream World, makers of Sew Steady tables, for providing us with a sewing table.

A big thank-you to Harriet's Treadle Arts for providing all the fabric, thread, and batting we could possibly use. Shopping after hours is such a joy! Also to our employees—Linda, Cindy, TJ, Georganne, Shar, and Kari—who kept the store going strong so we could stay home to write and sew for endless hours.

The authors take full responsibility for the contents of this book, including the technical accuracy of the information. Please direct any questions to quilt.academy.q.a@earthlink.net.

Contents

Preface

You are holding the first in a series of six books. The purpose of the series is to build your quiltmaking skills—from beginner to advanced—on a firm foundation. This first volume is to be used as a workbook. It contains a complete sequence of classes, lessons, exercises, and projects that will build your skills from one project to the next. We highly recommend that you make the quilts in the order presented, as we have placed them in order of complexity. Each quilt offers new challenges and involves new techniques that will help you continually build your skill level. We have chosen designs that are timeless and very adaptable to traditional fabrics as well as to more trendy fabric and color choices. Use these quilts to explore your color and style preferences.

This book and the next in the series deal with quilts made of strips and squares. By mastering the techniques presented in these first books, you will be laying a foundation for precise, high-quality piecing. There are hundreds of quilt designs based on strips and squares, so you can spend a long time exploring these stunning quilts before you jump into the more complex piecing featured in the following books.

> **note** *We do not address the quilting process in these books. The most thorough book available about machine quilting is my Heirloom Machine Quilting (see Resources, page 112). I strongly recommend that you study it as you are learning to piece and that you learn to do simple quilting as you progress with your quilt tops. Nothing is more satisfying than finishing the projects as you go. By the time you are into the more advanced techniques, your quilting will have evolved, and you will be creating wonderful quilts.*

A note from Harriet

What I have encountered in the past few years of teaching piecing is that there are many classes taught as projects, but the basic skills needed to really understand the *process* are severely lacking. Students come in having made several quilt tops but lacking cutting, sewing, and pressing skills. They know how to make an individual project, but they do not have the knowledge to apply general principles to other patterns they want to make.

In 2005, my daughter took over the management of Harriet's Treadle Arts—my quilt store, which I started in 1981 with my mother, also a quilter. Carrie grew up in the store and always loved fabric, but she was never interested in making quilts. Now in her early 30s, she is becoming more and more interested in sewing and quilting but has a different way of looking at the progression and style of quiltmaking. Whereas I love antique quilts and spend my time reproducing very old, very detailed quilts, Carrie wants to make the same traditional patterns in more up-to-date fabrics and easier quilting styles. As I get older, I have more time to spend on detail. She has less time to spend but still has the desire to create with the jazzy new fabrics available. We also see increasingly younger people coming into the store who are becoming interested in quilting and sewing but who have had no background, knowledge, or exposure to sewing.

Our plan is to walk you through a series of classes, lessons, and projects that will build one skill on another, so that when you have worked your way through the entire series of books you will be well on your way to being a master piecer. Each book in the series is like a year of college courses, from freshman to PhD candidate. After your "college education," you will never again be dependent on books and patterns, but will be able to draft or design anything you can dream up, *and* you will know how to piece—and quilt—it yourself! Following is a brief description of the books in the series.

Vol. 1—Freshman Year addresses the basic workspace, tools, equipment, and fabric needed to get you started. The first quilts presented utilize strips and squares, teaching you the most basic skills. With all the projects, more than just a "recipe" appears. The basics of drafting are introduced with each pattern, and every detail of cutting, sewing accurately, pressing, checking for size, and laying out for efficient piecing processes is covered.

Vol. 2—Sophomore Year addresses upgrading your workspace and adding tools and equipment as needed. We continue with quilts that use strips and squares for the design, but we add new settings and explore fun sashing and border ideas that really dress up simple blocks.

Vol. 3—Junior Year leads you into all forms of triangles, made with many different methods, including half-square and quarter-square triangle units as well as Flying Geese and pyramids. You will work through several quilts that help you build more skills with the more difficult piecing processes. A beautiful, complex Feathered Star quilt is the final project.

Vol. 4—Senior Year jumps into set-in piecing and all the fantastically complicated blocks, such as Seven Sisters and Lone Star, that feature it. By this time, your skill level will be up to the challenge, and you will be able to make some stunning quilts.

Vol. 5—Your Master's Year challenges your knowledge with the building of medallion quilts using the techniques and skills you have learned in the books up to this point.

Vol. 6—Your PhD Year presents projects with extremely challenging quilts—ones that you seldom find patterns for, such as Peony and Primrose Star.

Now, are you ready for the challenge? You can take your time with each book and really learn the fine art of quiltmaking. We hope you enjoy the journey with us and become a true master quilter.

Class 110

In this beginning class, we're going to give you the basics you need to know to get started, from setting up a simple sewing area to collecting the basic tools. This is the very first step in your quiltmaking adventure. We know it's dry stuff, but it's *really* important!

how to use this book

Because our approach to teaching the skills of quiltmaking is different from what anyone else has yet done, there are two ways to use this book. If, like Harriet, you want all the "meat and potatoes"—what to look for and do, how to set up everything before you start sewing—you can read ahead to get the more detailed information in this book. If, like Carrie, you want to get started making a quilt top and will gradually create a dedicated sewing, ironing, and cutting space as you need it, work your way through this book class by class, lesson by lesson. By the end, you will have a number of lovely quilt tops ready to quilt, and you'll be well on your way to being a quilter!

LESSON ONE: Setting up a sewing area

If you are just starting out, this lesson will give you an idea of the bare minimum you need in terms of work space to be able to create the quilt tops that we will make in this book. It may be daunting to think about all the equipment needed to start quilting if you are just beginning. If you already have a sewing room…great! You are ready to jump in and begin. However, while having a dedicated sewing space is nice, be assured that it is not really necessary for making a quilt. We'll show you how to set up a simple layout that will get you started. We'll give you more details about ergonomics and space requirements when you get to Class 140.

SEWING MACHINE AREA

Piecing does not require an extensive work area like machine quilting does. The rough minimum sewing space you need for making a quilt top is about 3 feet by 4 feet, mostly to your left and behind your sewing machine. If your machine is on a tabletop instead of in a cabinet, you will need a good support system around the machine. If you are sewing on a dining room or kitchen table, the photo shows a great setup for a sewing machine. It is easily taken apart and put away when the space is needed for other things.

Setup of a basic sewing area

If you cannot find someone to make a table like the one pictured on page 5, you can buy one that is cut to fit your machine, like the Sew Steady Portable Sewing Table by Dream World (which comes in several sizes).

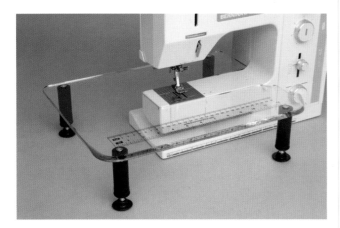

Sew Steady table

IRONING AREA

Your ironing board is a major workstation when you are piecing. Be sure that it is heavy, stable, and not warped. If yours has any of these issues, shop for a new one.

When ironing (even clothing), be aware that too much padding can lead to distortion. When you are piecing a quilt, inaccurate pressing of the pieces can ruin your project. A thin layer of 100% cotton batting (not more than ⅛ inch thick) makes an ideal ironing pad under the ironing board cover. A gridded ironing board cover is helpful. If the cover is stretched onto the board tight and straight, the lines of the grid can be used as guides to keep strips straight when pressing. See Class 140, Lesson Two, for more information about your pressing area page 39).

It can be difficult to handle larger pieces on an ironing board because of its shape. It's helpful to turn the ironing board around so you are working on the wider end.

tip Avoid using a Teflon ironing board cover. The slippery surface makes it hard for the fabric pieces to get a grip and create resistance for the iron. Also, the fabric does not dry after you have steamed or starched it. Cotton is preferable because cotton sticks to cotton and absorbs moisture, and a cotton ironing board cover will keep the pieces from sliding when you are ironing seams. It also allows the pieces to dry quickly between steaming and starching.

CUTTING AREA

Kitchen or laundry room counters, or even the top of the clothes dryer, are good places to set up a makeshift cutting area. Just make sure it's not too far from your sewing and ironing area.

Find a place that's at a comfortable height. If you are over 5 feet tall, about 36 inches is the best height. If you are under 5 feet tall, 32 inches or less will work for you. The main idea is that you do not want to lean over too much (ideally not at all) in order to be comfortable and to have the strength and power to cut the fabric cleanly and accurately. See Class 140, Lesson Two, page 39), for more information about ergonomics.

LESSON TWO:
Sewing machines

Of course, if you are going to learn to machine piece, you need a sewing machine. Today's sewing machine companies put a great deal of effort into making machines (even midline machines) that do everything, from straight stitch to digitized embroidery. The real story is that to excel at machine piecing, appliqué, and quilting, you need only a very basic machine. Few stitches beyond straight stitches are required, but there are some basic things you should consider when choosing a machine.

CHOOSING A SEWING MACHINE

We strongly advise you to avoid buying a cheap sewing machine at a big box store. It is best to choose a quality machine that not only gives you the features you need to start out but also allows you to grow into other techniques.

An excellent way to get a high-quality machine at an affordable price is to look for a good used machine. The used machines of today were the top-end machines of a few years ago. A reliable sewing machine dealer generally has trade-in machines that are worth looking at. Try to test drive as many models and brands as you can, and make sure you actually sew on the machine you like best before you buy it. Many newer computerized machines are difficult for new sewers to understand, and you will be frustrated because the machine is in control instead of you!

If you don't want to invest in a machine, borrowing one from a family member or a friend is a good way to get started. If you already have a machine (or you borrow one), take it to a qualified mechanic and have it cleaned, oiled, and adjusted.

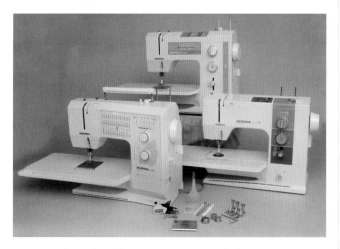

High-quality older equipment is a good place to start.

When you choose a machine, make sure that it is easy to regulate and understand. As you test it, note the sound of the machine, the placement of your foot on the foot control, the way the fabric feeds through the machine while you are sewing, the brightness of the machine light, and the machine's functions and accessories. Following are some functions and accessories that we recommend:

❊ *Fully adjustable stitch width and length capabilities.* Many machines have stitch length and width settings in predefined increments. This can hinder the ability to adjust the machine to any setting you need or want. A dial that has infinite settings between the numbers is ideal.

❊ *A bobbin with a case that inserts from the front of the machine* instead of dropping in from the top. These bobbin cases are more easily adjustable than the top, drop-in models. Placement of a seam guide (page 22) can be a problem with a drop-in system. Also consider bobbin size: the more thread it holds, the better.

❊ *A top tension adjustment dial that is easily accessible.* Numbers on the dial are also necessary.

❊ *Presser feet that change easily* and are stable (that do not wobble on the shank).

❊ *A feed-dog drop system that is easily accessible.*

❊ *A good-sized work surface around the machine,* or a tightly fitting portable sewing table that is made to go with the machine (see page 6).

❊ *A foot control* that is at a comfortable angle for your foot, so you can maintain control of the speed for long periods.

❊ *Presser feet and accessories* that really do the job:

- ¼″ foot
- Straight-stitch foot (available for Bernina)
- Seam guide bar (available for Bernina)
- Open-toe appliqué foot
- ¼″ round free-motion (darning) foot
- ¼″ round open-toe free-motion foot
- Walking foot
- Straight-stitch throat plate

The following are good used machines that you might want to look for and try out.

❊ Bernina mechanical machines – Models 930, 1020, 1030

❊ Bernina computerized machines – Models 1090, 1130, 1230, 1260

❊ Pfaff – Models 1475 through 7570

❊ Viking – Lily, Rose, 1+

PRESSER FEET

The importance of presser feet cannot be overstated. They affect your view as you sew, the feeding of the fabric, and the accuracy of your seams. Most sewing machines come with a variety of presser feet, but most of these are for dressmaking and do not work for the narrow seam allowances used in patchwork.

In the past few years, we have seen presser feet developed especially for piecing ¼″ seams. A universal ¼″ foot is the Little Foot, developed by Lynn Graves. This foot is designed to be a perfect ¼″ on the right side of the needle. The foot has ¼″ markings on the side to indicate the needle position: ¼″ behind the needle for starting the seam; a line directly across from the needle; and ¼″ in front of the needle, to indicate when to stop ¼″ from the edge. This foot is available in several shank sizes to adapt to most machines and is a good choice if your machine does not have a ¼″ foot available.

Various ¼″ piecing feet

Most sewing machine companies have made ¼" feet for their specific brands for several years now, and the theory is that on all ¼" feet, it's exactly ¼" from the needle to the right-hand edge of the presser foot. However, because these feet aren't necessarily totally accurate, not all quilters like using them.

Harriet's favorite foot is the Bernina #13, an old-fashioned straight-stitch foot like the one found on the Singer Featherweight. This foot has a very narrow toe on the right side and a wider one on the left. A guide bar can be placed in the back of the foot and positioned to whatever width from the foot you want the seam. The guide bar allows you to see the fabric pass to the side of the toe and watch it ride alongside the guide bar. This gives you much more control as the fabric passes under the foot and will automatically help clean up many accuracy issues in piecing.

hint When the Bernina #13 foot is set up with the guide bar, you can cut off the extra bar that extends to the left of the presser foot, thus making it a very compact, usable foot. The bar extension won't hurt anything, but it's cumbersome.

After being introduced to this foot by Sharyn Craig, Harriet has never gone back to the ¼" foot. Unfortunately, not every machine manufacturer makes this foot, but it is worth looking into.

For more about presser feet and accurate seams, see Class 130, page 20.

hint Not all sewing machines have this foot available because the manufacturers have made their straight-stitch feet wide like zigzag feet, with a single hole where the needle passes through. This foot does not meet our needs.

STRAIGHT-STITCH THROAT PLATE

The throat plate is the metal piece that surrounds the feed dog. The standard throat plate on a modern machine has an oval opening that accommodates a zigzag stitch, which doesn't work well for piecing. The oval hole allows the needle to push fabric down with it, and the stitch may not be made cleanly. Also, strips tend to veer away from the edge of the seam guide as you approach the ends, so it is hard to keep them straight and even while sewing.

A straight-stitch plate will help eliminate this problem. This plate's opening is too small to allow the fabric to enter with the needle. Straight-stitch machines such as Singer Featherweights make perfect stitches, and many quilters still prefer to piece on their old machines because of the stitch quality.

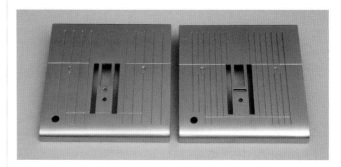

Straight-stitch and zigzag throat plates

LESSON THREE: Rotary cutters and cutting mats

The variety of rotary cutters and mats available today is amazing. When Harriet started quilting in the 1970s, rotary cutters had not been invented yet! Once they hit the market in the early 1980s, they revolutionized cutting fabric for quilting.

ROTARY CUTTERS

A rotary cutter is like a round razor blade with a handle. Rotary cutters are available in 18mm, 28mm, 45mm, 60mm, and 65mm blade sizes. There are several brands of rotary cutters, each with slightly different features. We suggest that you go to various quilting stores and ask to test-drive the brands and styles of cutters they carry. You will find that there is a vast difference in how they are held and where the pressure is applied as you cut with them.

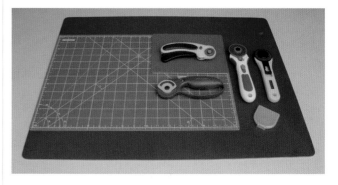

Rotary cutting supplies

Cutting fabric correctly is critical to good piecing, and cutting is where beginners have the most difficulty. If your cutter does not fit your hand properly, or you can't apply even and steady pressure to the blade for the entire length of the cut, the cut will not go through the fabric layers and/or the edge will not be cut cleanly.

> *hint* Please don't let the preferences of your friends, your mom or grandma, or a salesclerk influence what you buy. Try what they like and recommend, but form your own opinion after trying several different cutters.

We recommend starting with the 45mm size. It is easy to cut with, goes through four layers of fabric easily, rides above the thickness of a rotary ruler, and comes in models with many different shapes and handles. This is the only size you need to get started.

> ### safety note
> Be very careful when using rotary cutters. They are razor sharp! Make it a habit to close your cutter every time you lay it down. Never leave a cutter lying around, open or closed, where small children can get hold of it.

HOLDING A CUTTER PROPERLY

Many books, as well as the instructions on cutter packages, suggest that you hold the cutter with a closed fist. This method doesn't help direct the energy of your arm and hand onto the blade. Instead, let the handle of the cutter rest comfortably in the palm of your hand. Your index finger should extend forward, resting on the grooved space at the top edge of the handle (if the cutter has this). Your thumb should be on one side of the handle, and the other three fingers should curl gently around the other side.

Holding a rotary cutter properly

Always cut *away* from your body. The muscles you use when pushing are stronger than those you use when pulling. You also eliminate the possibility of losing control of the cutter and hurting yourself!

MAINTENANCE

The rotary cutter blade is razor sharp when new, but after dozens of cuts it can start to dull. A dull blade requires more force than a sharp blade to do the same work, which can be tiring and can make your cutting inaccurate. Make sure you have one or two new blades on hand.

Several newer cutters on the market have easy blade-changing systems. When changing the blade on one of the other cutters, lay out the parts in the order you take them off the handle. Wipe any lint from the back of the handle area that the blade rests on. Change the blade, making sure you select only a single blade if you purchased a multipack, and reassemble the parts in reverse order. You will notice that the new blade has a thin film of oil on it. Do not wipe this off, because it helps lubricate the blade while cutting.

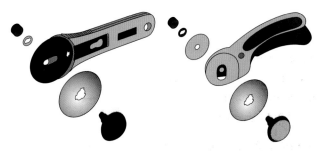

Lay out parts of cutter in order as you disassemble it.

ROTARY CUTTING MATS

The cutting surface is just as important as the cutter you use. The mat allows you to press down on the cutter and let the blade sink slightly into the surface of the mat. Rotary cutting mats come in different sizes and materials, so you'll need to try a few to find your preferences as to thickness, hardness, and ease of cutting.

✻ Three-layer mats (made by Elan and Olfa) are made of two layers of PVC plastic, with a softer center layer. They are "self-healing," meaning that the cuts do not stay in the surface. Either side can be cut on. Store them flat and away from heat; they will warp if exposed to a heat source or left in a hot car.

✱ The harder, thinner version of the three-layer mat (made by Olfa, Omnigrid, and Ginger) feels flatter and harder when cutting. This type is also self-healing, and either side can be used to cut.

✱ Soft plastic mats are solid translucent white plastic with a textured side (the cutting side) and a smooth side. They are usually not self-healing—the cutter may leave marks on the surface. Cuts can be smoothed with emery cloth or very fine sandpaper, but over time the board can become grooved and will distort the path of your cutter. It also dulls blades faster.

✱ A few mats (made by June Tailor and Fiskars) are very hard plastic and have a textured cutting surface. Only one side of these mats can be used for cutting, and, of all the mats, these seem to be the hardest to cut accurately on.

Rotary mats come in a variety of sizes. The most versatile size, 18″ × 24″, is what we recommend to start. If or when you get a large cutting table, the 24″ × 36″ mat is more efficient for doing a lot of cutting. There are also small mats that are handy for quick trimming at the machine and for taking to classes. Finally, there are mats that attach to ironing surfaces for use in very confined spaces.

WORKING WITHOUT THE GRID LINES

All mats come with a 1-inch grid printed on one side. Many books will tell you to work with this grid, but rarely do the mat lines match the lines of your ruler, and you will have too many lines to look at. Therefore, work on the solid side only, and rely on your ruler for accurate measurements.

LESSON FOUR: Ruler basics

Along with rotary cutters and cutting mats, rulers make up the foundation of the rotary revolution. A clear, accurate ruler is as important to guiding the cutter as a sharp blade is to cutting. There are many different rulers available for both general and specialty use. Rotary rulers are made of thick, clear acrylic and have lines and numbers evenly spaced across them. The number of lines and their spacing varies between brands, as do the color and thickness of the lines. Rulers that have numbers running in both directions are easy for both right- and left-handed quilters to use.

RULER BRANDS AND CHARACTERISTICS

When deciding on a ruler brand, keep the following in mind:

✱ **Do not change brands of rulers in the middle of a project!** We cannot stress enough how important this point is. The measurements marked on the different brands will vary slightly. Find a brand you like, and stick with it.

✱ Make sure that the brand you choose comes in a fairly large selection of sizes and shapes.

✱ Be sure to place the rulers on top of both dark and light fabrics to check that the color of the lines shows enough to enable you to work with the ruler easily and accurately.

✱ Check the thickness of the printed lines. The thicker the line, the greater the chance that you will measure and cut inaccurately.

✱ It is handy to have a ruler marked with a 45°-angle line, as well as 30°- and 60°-angle lines.

✱ Some brands have a ½″ measure on one side and end. Be sure to keep this in mind when cutting. The ½″ is added so that you only have to think about the finished strip size you need—the ½″ seam allowance is already added. This can cause trouble if you don't pay attention to it.

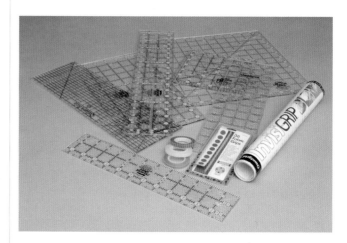

Variety of rulers in basic sizes

BASIC STARTER SIZES

To start with, you will need a limited number of rulers. Good sizes to start with are any combination of the following:

> **note** Some brands add a ½" measure to two sides of their rulers; others do not. The sizes below are the general sizes of the rulers, whether the ½" is added or not. Creative Grids all have ½" added. Some Omnigrid rulers do and some don't. It would be advisable to be consistent in this when buying rulers.

* 2½" × 12½"
* 3½" × 18½"
* 4" × 12" or 14"
* 6½" × 12" or 18½"
* 6½" square
* 9½" square
* 12½" square
* 18½" square

The four "bare-bones" basic sizes you will need to make most of the quilts in this book are a 2½" × 12½", a 4" × 12" or 14", a 6½" × 12" or 18½", and a 6½" square. Add the other sizes once you get into adding borders, and for continuing in your quilting.

> **tip** While it may be tempting to go to a large chain store and use a 40%-off coupon to buy these basic supplies, we highly recommend that you shop your local quilt shop. It will usually carry a larger variety of "quilter-friendly" notions and tools, and the salespeople will explain the features and uses of the tools to you.

ACCURATE MEASURING GUIDES

Before investing in a ruler, test-drive several brands and sizes, especially to see how well you can read them. Many quilters find that certain color markings or too many lines make cutting very confusing and fatiguing. Be sure that you can easily read the measurements and follow a line the length of the ruler without your eyes blurring. (Confusion in reading the lines will lead to inaccurate cutting.) Strips of self-stick plastic called Glow-Line Tape can be placed along a measure line to help you with ruler placement.

SLIPPAGE-STOP PRODUCTS

Ruler slippage is a common problem when cutting. Quilter's Rule rulers have a molded side with a raised grid to prevent slippage. Creative Grid rulers have built-in grips on the back along the sides.

Some products can be placed on the back of any ruler. Invisi-Grip by Omnigrid "disappears" but stops a lot of the slippage. Fabric Grips by Collins are small sandpaper circles with self-adhesive backing. EZ Clear Fabric Grabbers are clear, but thicker. They really grab the fabric, but they make the ruler sit above the surface of the fabric.

If you don't want something permanently stuck to your ruler, you can use small pieces of plastic shelf liner or rug backing. These stick to the ruler when you apply pressure but peel off easily.

We have found that slippage often occurs when using a ruler that is wider than needed. Use the narrowest ruler you can for the size of strips you are cutting, and slippage will be less of a problem.

> **note** All the factors we have discussed in this class affect your ability to cut easily and accurately. The table height must be correct, the mat a correct size, the rotary cutter comfortable, and the cutter blade sharp. If you have problems cutting, consider all of the above. Your hand position on the ruler is dependent on how you stand at the table and how much pressure you can apply to the ruler. We will walk you through this process in Class 120 page 19).

All right! You made it through the nuts-and-bolts section—now on to fabric!

Class 120

LESSON ONE: All about fabric

One of the most fun aspects of being a quilter is buying and collecting fabric. If you have not yet been bitten by the fabric bug, get ready. Quilters buy fabric just because they *have* to own a piece of it! It is like collecting artwork. Each fabric has a beauty of its own, and when you combine it with several others, the WOW! factor kicks in. Many of us lose sleep planning the quilts that our fabrics inspire us to make.

Falling in love with and buying fabric is only the beginning. Choosing the right fabrics and preparing them properly is essential in order to keep fabrics and quilts durable and vibrant for years.

In this class, you'll learn the basics about fabric selection and preparation. In Class 160, we'll get to the aesthetics—color, prints, and so forth.

When choosing fabrics for quiltmaking, fiber content, thread count, shrinkage, and colorfastness all need to be taken into consideration. We strongly recommend using only high-quality 100% cotton fabrics. It's also essential that your fabric be straight and on-grain in order for your finished quilt top to be successful. You'll learn all about these factors in this class.

> *note* As this series of lessons progresses, we will delve deeper into the subject of textiles. Harriet's book on textiles for quiltmakers, entitled From Fiber to Fabric, explores the science of making fabric, batting, and thread. If you are interested in the nitty-gritty of quiltmaking products, this book is a necessary read (see Resources, page 112).

FABRIC BASICS

Selvage – the lengthwise edges of the fabric, usually from ¼ to ½ inch wide. The selvage ensures that the edges of the fabric will not tear when the cloth undergoes the stresses and strains of the printing and finishing processes.

Lengthwise grain – runs parallel to the selvage and has very little stretch. Also known as the *warp yarns*.

Crosswise grain – runs perpendicular to the selvage and has more stretch than the lengthwise grain. Also called *filling* or *weft yarns*.

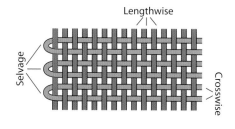

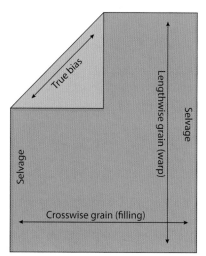

Position of fabric grains

Bias – the 45° angle to both sets of yarns. It has the most stretch.

Thread count – the number of threads in a square inch of cloth, both lengthwise and crosswise. Quilting fabric is an even-weave fabric, meaning there are an equal number of yarns in both directions. Quality fabrics for quiltmaking run from 60 × 60 to 76 × 76 yarns per square inch. The fewer yarns in the count, the heavier and beefier the fabric will feel. The higher the thread count, the finer and tighter the fabric feels.

FABRIC GRAIN

It is very important that you work with fabrics that are on-grain. Not all fabrics that you buy will be perfectly on-grain, but most can be straightened and put back on-grain once you get them home. We'll explain how in Exercise: Realigning fabric grain (page 15). This brings us to the subject of tearing versus cutting fabric from the bolt.

TEARING VERSUS CUTTING OFF THE BOLT

When you buy fabric, it will either be cut or torn off the bolt, depending on your quilt shop owner's preference. Some quilters favor one approach and some the other. The most common reason for the alignment problem is that the fabric is wrapped onto the bolt unevenly. Whether it is cut or torn can affect whether you get enough fabric for your project.

Cutting. If a fabric is cut off the bolt at a perfect 90° angle to the selvage, you might think you have the exact amount you need. However, consider whether the fabric is coming off the bolt on-grain crosswise. You will need to look very closely to see how the filling yarns (crosswise, selvage to selvage) align with the warp yarns (parallel to the selvage). Are they perfectly straight and even with the cut, or do they run off the cut edge at an angle? Once cut, do the yarns of the crosswise grain unravel evenly from edge to edge? Or do they stop somewhere along the cut?

Different degrees of off-grain shown by tearing

Left: Fabric torn from bolt showing edges out of alignment
Right: Same fabric cut from bolt—uneven edges aren't visible

Cutting an off-grain fabric off the bolt can often add up to a large loss. Once you've straightened it at home, you may find yourself short of the yardage you need for the project. If you detect this at the store, you'll need to purchase up to ¼ yard extra just for straightening.

Tearing. If a fabric is torn from the bolt, you automatically know if the fabric is on-grain or not. You will have exactly the same usable length on each selvage edge, even though the ends do not line up.

When the fabric is torn, some of the threads can turn over, exposing the backside that has not been saturated or printed with dye. This is more prevalent in fabrics with low (60 × 60) thread count. If the fabric is torn, this damaged area is generally added to the yardage you're buying at each end. Therefore, when you cut away the damaged areas after straightening, you'll be left with the exact yardage you purchased.

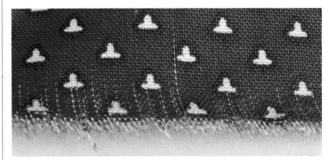
Turned threads caused by low thread count and tearing

If you find that the torn edges of the fabric on the bolt are up to 3 inches off-grain, feel the "hand" of the fabric. If it is soft and pliable, you'll most likely get the grain realigned with little effort. If the fabric feels stiff, reconsider buying it—stiff fabric can be next to impossible to straighten. Also, if the bolt is labeled "perma-press," the fabric might be a bit harder to straighten.

PRINT/GRAIN ALIGNMENT

If fabric is printed off-grain, you need to consider how you are using the fabric and whether this will affect the finished quilt. Too often, you won't notice this problem until the quilt is finished and you see that the off-grain fabric wavers.

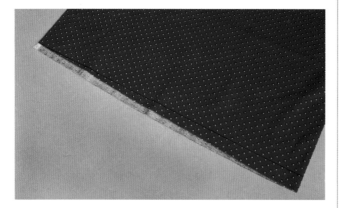

Line shows print is off-grain crosswise.

General guidelines for this issue are as follows:

❁ If the pieces are cut small enough that the off-grain print isn't noticeable, you can cut on-grain, off-print.

❁ If you are planning to use the fabric for larger blocks and pieces, cutting on-print, off-grain will give the most appealing look.

❁ Cutting borders on the lengthwise grain can help minimize the problem.

Left: Block cut on-grain, off-print. Right: Block cut on-print, off-grain

If you're thinking of using an off-grain print for sashing or borders and the problem would be obvious, you would need to cut on-print. However, because borders should be on the straight grain for stability (and, in the case of wallhangings, to make the piece hang straight), you might need to choose a different fabric.

LESSON TWO:
Washing your fabric
THE "BIG DEBATE": PREWASH OR NOT?

The "big debate" is whether to prewash all your fabrics as soon as you get them home, or to store them new and make the choice whether to wash them or not depending on the project. Like everything else, this can be a multifaceted issue. It has to do with how you work, as well as the style of quilting you develop. It also involves colorfastness and other fabric issues. Because it can be a complex question, we don't want to simply say, "Do (or don't) prewash, and everything will be okay." That might set you up for potential problems in the future. Therefore, we are introducing some concepts that you might want to keep in mind as you begin to buy fabric. We will expand on this topic with each of the books in this series.

PREWASHING

Many quilters prewash everything as it comes in the door, believing that this will take care of color bleeding and shrinkage. However, you can't tell if a fabric has a colorfastness problem just by washing it. In fact, incorrect prewashing can actually *cause* stress, fading, or bleeding in fabrics. As for shrinkage of the finished quilt, you will find that it is actually dictated by the batting and the spacing of the quilting stitches, not by the fabric.

The decision to prewash or not will be based on your personal preferences as you learn to quilt. Many quilters work with prewashed fabric because they deal with many colors and scraps, often shared among several quilters. You may want to prewash if you prefer the soft "hand" of washed fabric, or if you prefer a less textured look to the quilt when it is finished and laundered.

You will find that piecing with prewashed fabric presents a few problems. Prewashed fabric is soft and has less body than new fabric, so it can be a bit harder to cut accurately. When you are sewing, the pressure of the presser foot can distort the pieces slightly. Also, pressed seams tend not to be as flat and crisp as with unwashed fabric. Starching prewashed fabric can help. However, do not starch fabric before storing it. Starch can invite bugs such as silverfish and moths to take up residence in your stash, so starch only the yardage you need for a particular project. Starch it when you straighten the grain to give it stability for cutting and sewing, and when pressing, for sharper edges on the pressed seams.

note If you find that you are allergic to the finish on a fabric, or you develop a skin rash from working with nonwashed fabrics, then by all means, prewash!

NONWASHING

Some quilters prefer to store all their fabric just as it comes off the bolt, and then to prewash or not for a given quilt project depending on the look they want for the finished quilt. For example, if all your fabric is prewashed, but you decide to make a reproduction 1930s quilt, the finished quilt will not have the right texture and look. That vintage look comes from the shrinkage of the fabric and batting together. The shrinkage is what makes the older quilts soft, warm, and cuddly. However, if you want to make a contemporary wall quilt with no texture, prewashing might be the best solution. If you do not prewash everything as you buy it, your options are always open and your fabric stash is very versatile.

Neither way of handling fabric is right or wrong. It's as simple as deciding on your preferences and work styles. Try working with both washed and nonwashed fabrics. Start out by storing your new fabric unwashed. If you find that over time, you're constantly washing every piece, you will probably want to switch to prewashing. If, however, you find that you need the choice of nonwashed fabric for some of your projects, or you just prefer the feel of working with it, you may want to store all your fabric unwashed, and wash it when you're ready to use it. The bottom line is that you need to take responsibility for your decisions and make them based on fact, not on guesswork or because "someone told me I had to."

tip For beginners, Carrie recommends sticking with safe colors to lessen your headaches. Mediums, lights, pastels, and multicolor prints are generally free from most color transference problems. Avoid using two highly contrasting colors, such as red and white, as well as batiks and very dark, rich colors.

note Again, if you want the complete story on fabrics right now, consult Harriet's book From Fiber to Fabric.

We feel that at this point, all that detailed information would be overwhelming. However, if we simply tell you, "Prewash (or not), and everything will be okay," that would not be honest, and it would set you up for potential problems with your quilts in the future. So, we have introduced some concepts for you to keep in mind as you begin buying fabric.

Right now we know you just want to jump in and get started. But as you expand your skills and your interest continues, you will be ready to take the time to deal with the care of textiles in a knowledgeable way. So we will expand on this topic with each book in this series.

LESSON THREE:
Preparing fabric

Your fabric must be prepared properly before you cut it, so that the units sew and press accurately. When working with strips, as we are in this book—whether they are for strip piecing, sashings, or borders—the trueness of the fabric's grain is a major factor in how well your quilt top behaves. If the grainline along the edge of the strips varies by more than a few threads, there is potential for stretching and distortion. In this class, we explain the right way to realign fabric that is off-grain.

❋ EXERCISE: REALIGNING FABRIC GRAIN

Supplies:

Pins

Iron

Faultless Heavy spray starch

Materials:

½ yard 100% cotton fabric

Many people believe that by pulling the fabric on the bias opposite to the direction it is off, they can straighten the fabric. However, if you examine a piece of fabric that has been pulled in this way, you'll see that the yarns have been misaligned and pulled out of square. *A better way to realign the fabric grain is to press a new center fold into the fabric.*

1. If your fabric is not already torn, begin by tearing each end of the yardage to find the crosswise grain. (Work in short yardages of ½ yard or less.) Make a ½″ clip in the fold at least 2½″ from each end of the fabric and grasp both sides of the cut at the fold. Tear quickly to prevent stretching.

Start with a ½″ cut to tear fabric.

> *tip* Tearing a strip at least 2½ inches wide off your fabric will enable you to cut pieces for your quilts from that strip later, if needed. Tearing narrower strips may result in having to tear a second or third strip in order to get the fabric to tear cleanly from selvage to selvage. It is better to tear a big strip to start with and have it wide enough to use later than to waste a smaller piece of fabric.

2. Open the fabric so it lies flat on your ironing board and spray it with water to dampen it lightly. If you have prewashed the fabric, you can do this step while the fabric is still damp. The sizing must be damp in order to allow the yarns to move back to their original position.

3. Press to remove the original center fold. Iron the fabric dry. If you have prewashed the fabric, now is a good time to start applying starch to build body and stability back into the fabric.

4. Fold the fabric in half from selvage to selvage and pin the 2 selvage edges together. A can of heavy spray starch is helpful here. Lightly spray with starch and use your fingers to coax the fabric to lie flat.

Fold in half and pin selvages together to start straightening process.

> *tip* Starch works like a muscle relaxant for fabric, helping it "relax" into the new shape. Our favorite is Faultless Heavy spray starch. It seems to add the most crispness without flaking or scorching. Make sure your iron is not set beyond the cotton setting. If the iron is too hot, the starch will scorch and stick to the bottom of the iron.

5. To create a new center fold, press toward the center, working from the torn edge and selvage down. Use one hand on the iron, and the other to smooth the fabric as you press. You are coaxing the fabric back into alignment, so be patient and light-handed. Steam can also be helpful in this process, but don't use steam after you have applied starch.

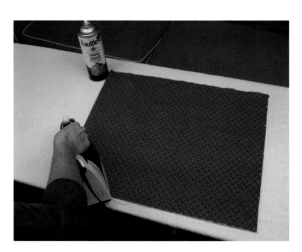

Using iron to press fold

6. If you have someone around who can work with you, this job can be very efficient. As one person holds the fabric at the selvage corners and the other pulls at each end of the center fold, the fabric will automatically realign into a new center fold.

An extra pair of hands makes fast work of realigning grain.

7. Once you have established a new center fold, turn the fabric over and press the other side, checking for folds and distortions. Fold the fabric in half crosswise again.

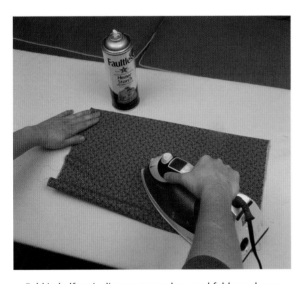

Fold in half again, line up torn edges, and fold to selvage.

8. Check to see that the torn edges again align. If not, repeat the process. A few threads' variance is acceptable here. Once this final alignment is achieved, the fabric is ready for cutting.

LESSON FOUR: Working properly with a ruler

Before cutting strips, you must establish a straight edge on the fabric. In addition, check the following three things before you actually cut the fabric.

❋ First, make sure your fabric is well pressed. Take a minute and iron the fabric to eliminate sharp creases where the fabric has been folded in storage (not the creases you pressed in when straightening). Pressing your fabric carefully at this point will make it easier to cut now and to sew later.

❋ Second, make sure your cutting mat is on a firm, flat surface that allows plenty of room for your fabric and tools. A solid wood table has no give and works best to support the mat and the pressure of cutting. (Most newer lightweight plastic folding tables are too spongy.)

❋ Third, check how your fabric is folded. Fold it wrong sides together so that the selvage edges match up. Fold it a second time so that the fold matches up with the selvages. The fabric is now 11″ wide (this is the folded size that you get once you straighten the grain as described on page 17.

note *Many quilters prefer not to make the second fold, but work with the fabric folded once, selvage to selvage, making the fabric 22 inches wide. This may eliminate some of the problems with bends in the fabric strips, but the ruler is apt to slip when cutting such a long length. We suggest that you try both ways to see which feels most comfortable and gives you the most accurate results. Remember that a narrow ruler could eliminate much of the problem.*

A small, narrow ruler is more manageable when cutting strips. Choose a ruler that is several inches longer than the folded fabric. The narrower the ruler, the less likely it is to slip while you are cutting. If you are cutting narrow strips, a 2½″- or 3½″-wide ruler is adequate.

We recommend that you work with the lines of the ruler and avoid using the grid lines printed on the cutting mat. If possible, turn the mat over to the plain side.

Position the ruler on the fabric, and place the ring finger of the hand holding the ruler against the ruler's outside edge. This helps brace the ruler so it doesn't slip while you are cutting.

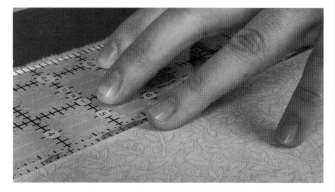

Placement of ring finger against edge to help prevent slippage

When cutting, you can walk your hand up the length of the ruler to keep it straight and accurate, keeping your finger against the edge of the ruler.

❋ EXERCISE: PREPARING FABRIC TO CUT STRIPS

Supplies:

Rotary cutter, mat, and ruler

Materials:

Straightened fabric, folded to be 11″ wide, from Exercise: Realigning fabric grain (page 15)

1. To clean up the torn fabric edge and establish a straight edge, position a cross line of the ruler on the folded edge of the fabric. This fold should be closest to you, with the selvage edge at the top. If you are right-handed, the fabric will be positioned so that it extends to the left. If you are left-handed, the fabric will extend to the right.

Position of fabric if left-handed

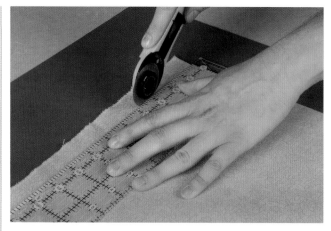

Position of fabric if right-handed

2. Your arm should be extended comfortably at about a 45° angle to your body. Hold the cutter with the blade next to the ruler. You should be able to make one clean cutting action across the fabric, applying enough pressure to cut through all the layers, but not so much that you cut into the mat. Do not saw back and forth on the fabric; this will result in a rough, choppy edge.

3. Keep the long edge of the ruler close to the torn edge of the fabric and a cross line of the ruler on the double fold. This aligns the ruler at both the fold and the edge to be cut. Cut off the torn edge.

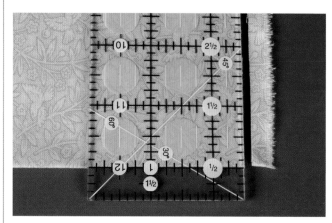

Align cross lines on ruler.

LESSON FIVE:
Cutting straight strips

Now that you have a properly aligned piece of fabric with a straight edge, you're ready to cut strips.

✳ EXERCISE: CUTTING STRIPS

Supplies:

Rotary cutter, mat, and ruler

Materials:

Straightened and trimmed fabric from previous exercise

1. Once you have cut off the torn edge, the fabric will now need to be turned 180°, so that the bulk of the fabric is on the same side as the hand you cut with.

2. To cut strips, position the ruler on top of the fabric, measuring in from the cut edge. Align the line of the measurement you desire with the cut edge, extending the ruler that amount into the body of the fabric. Make sure that the horizontal lines of the ruler align with the fold of the fabric perfectly, and that the vertical measurement line is running exactly along the cut edge.

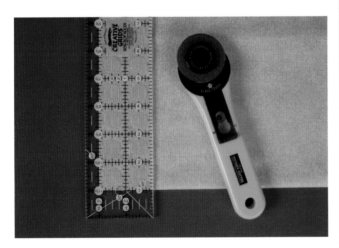

Position ruler to prepare to cut strips.

3. Unfold the first fabric strip you cut and check the center fold. If the strip is straight, you know the fabric is folded properly. If it has a V at the fold, your strips will continue to be bent unless you re-press the piece of fabric and make sure everything is even. If the ruler is not aligned perfectly with both the fold and the cut edge, you'll also get V's in every strip.

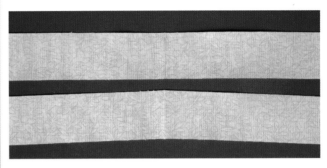

Straight strip and strip with V

4. As you continue to cut strips, be sure that the ruler remains exactly aligned with the fabric—checking both the cut edge and the fold. You can readily see when anything is out of alignment, as the fabric will no longer be perpendicular to the ruler. Check that you are using the same side of the printed line every time you align the ruler.

5. After cutting 3 or 4 strips, check again for straightness. If there is any V to the strips, realign the fabric piece and square it up again. The importance of this step cannot be overstressed. Too often we assume that everything is okay, only to find after cutting that all the strips are bent and therefore difficult to work with.

> *note* If you have several strips with V's, you can cut across them at the fold, and they will be usable as two shorter strips.

Double-check that your strips are all EXACTLY the same width. Take time to double-check which side of the ruler line you are aligning with. The simple act of changing sides of a line can cause a cut that is threads wider or narrower, making a difference in the width of the strip. Cutting is the first step toward accurate piecing. If the strip width varies by only a few threads, it will continually add up to misfit pieces.

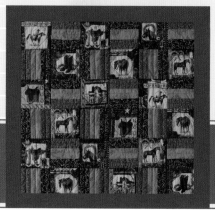

Class 130

You are actually going to get to sew in this class! Once you learn to sew accurate seam allowances and press properly, you will be ready to work on the small sampler quilt that Carrie designed as she took the classes in this series we teach at our store.

LESSON ONE:
Why ¼″ seams don't work

For years the quilt world has been obsessed by the myth of the ¼″ seam allowance. By believing that a ¼″ seam allowance is sacred, we have lost the ability to make perfect-sized quilt blocks.

One of the primary goals of this book is to help you achieve the correct size *block* instead of worrying about the size of the seam allowance. Making accurate-sized blocks is not all about the measurement of the seam or the foot on your machine—although these, as well as other factors, do affect the final finished size of the block. As you will eventually find out from doing the exercises in this class, you must work back from your finished sewn units and adjust your seam allowances to achieve an accurate-sized block. Read on and find out *why* the ¼″ seam does not work.

THREAD AND NEEDLES

THREADS

The relationship of thread weight to seam allowance width is an important factor in accurate sewing. Traditionally, quilters have pieced with 50-weight three-ply 100% cotton sewing thread, an appropriate weight for quilt fabrics. Thread size should be as fine as possible, consistent with the strength requirements of the seam. The "50" designates the *yarn count* of the thread, or the *weight and diameter*. The "three" indicates the number of *plies* twisted together. The higher the first number, the finer the thread. The more plies, the stronger the thread.

Variety of threads

The problem you encounter when you use 50/3 thread with a ¼″ foot and sew a *perfect* ¼″ seam is that there is no allowance for the weight of the thread and the bend of the fabric as you press the seam. You will find that *the seam allowance is the perfect size, but the finished unit is too small.*

In recent years, quilters have started using two-ply embroidery thread to piece their quilts because it is so fine that it does not create bulk in a seam and therefore, with a ¼″ foot, will produce accurate-sized units. We ask that you please think twice about doing this. Three-ply thread is needed for strength in the seam. Two-ply threads are too weak to hold up under the weight and wear and tear of a quilt, especially if the quilt is not quilted heavily.

A fairly new thread size on the market—60/3, manufactured by Presencia Hilaturas (Staple Fibre), a thread manufacturer from Spain, and introduced to Harriet through Carrie's master's study in textiles—solves this problem. The 60 weight makes it a very fine thread, but the three plies make it very strong in relation to the fineness. This thread is an excellent choice if you want to work with your ¼″ foot because it buys back the space taken by a heavier thread and the bend of the fabric when pressing. It also allows you to sew with a smaller needle, which eliminates the fabric distortion that larger needles can cause. Be sure that you always use 100% cotton thread in your quilts.

NEEDLE SIZES AND TYPES

The right needle is critical for a smooth stitch. Use only high-quality needles, and start each new project with a new needle. Check your sewing machine manual for the recommended type and brand of needle.

For now, universal-point needles will serve you just fine. If you use 50/3 thread, it is recommended that you use an 80/12 needle. If you choose the 60/3 Presencia, a 70/10 or 75/11 is the correct size.

Thread weight	Needle size
50/3 threads	75/11 or 80/12 needles
60/3 threads	70/10 or 75/11 needles

CHECKING PRESSER FOOT AND NEEDLE ACCURACY

In Class 110 we introduced you to the ¼″ foot. However, there is some discrepancy in the accuracy of the ¼″ feet that come with machines. The theory is that the needle is *exactly* ¼″ from the right-hand edge of the presser foot.

We recommend that you check the accuracy of the needle position yourself by placing a piece of ¼″ (4-squares-to-the-inch) graph paper under the presser foot and carefully lowering the needle until it goes into the paper on a line. Check that the right edge of the presser foot is exactly on the next ¼″ line.

If the edge of the foot does not fall exactly on the graph-paper line, the problem is generally *not* with the width of the foot but with the position of the needle. We assume that the needle is always exactly centered with the center of the foot, but often it is not. If the needle is too far to the left, you will be taking a slightly wider seam; if it is a bit to the right, the seam will be narrower. Using a seam guide (see page 23) will help eliminate problems.

Using graph paper to measure for ¼″

> *note* Some people suggest moving the needle position to the right to create an accurate seam allowance measurement. We strongly recommend that you avoid this practice because an off-center needle is mentally challenging to work with and can cause problems if your needle inadvertently gets moved to another position. Also, if you use a straight-stitch throat plate (see page 8), your needle must be in the center position.

HINTS FOR ACCURATE SEWING

Here are a few things to check when setting up your sewing machine:

❋ Check your body position when sitting at your machine. You should be facing the presser foot straight on when you align the fabric with the edge of the foot. If your body is angled, your perception of the edge of the fabric and the edge of the foot will be incorrect, and your seams will be less accurate.

❋ Be aware of the time of day and the position of the light around your work. If you start piecing in the morning with natural light on your left side and finish up at night with artificial light above you, your eyes are apt to see the edge of the foot differently. Keep the light consistent at all times if possible.

❋ Check that the foot is stable on the machine. Many clip-on feet wobble as you sew, and this play in the foot position will affect the accuracy of the seams. This is especially true if the foot has a little guide built onto the right side of it. These guides aren't always an accurate ¼" to start with, and any movement while sewing will throw off your seam allowance just enough to cause problems.

❋ Check the fabric position. If you see a bit of fabric beyond the right side of the ¼" foot, you are taking too wide a seam. If you don't see the edge of the fabric, where are you looking to guide the fabric under the foot? Is it going through the machine straight?

LESSON TWO:
Measuring for accuracy

MEASURING FOR ACCURATE PLACEMENT

There are several ways to ensure that a seam guide is positioned accurately. One of the cleverest tools to come along in quite a while is the Perkins Dry Goods Perfect Piecing Seam Guide. This little ruler allows you to mark your sewing machine for a consistent and accurate seam allowance every time. It actually measures a *scant* ¼", which allows for the weight of the thread and the bend of the fabric in each seam. It will also check the accuracy of the needle position in relation to the edge of the foot.

Place your needle in the hole of the Seam Guide ruler. Lower the presser foot to hold the Seam Guide ruler firmly in place, and straighten the Seam Guide ruler so it is parallel with the edge of the throat plate. Place the seam guide of your choice (see page 23) against the side of the Seam Guide ruler to mark a perfect scant ¼". Remove the Seam Guide ruler.

Placing tape alongside ruler

As stated earlier, using ¼" graph paper is another very accurate way to measure. Place the needle on a grid line of the graph paper. If the side of the foot does not match the next grid line to the right exactly, use a seam guide or piece of tape to mark the correct position.

If you use a ruler, be consistent as to which side of the line you put the needle on, and make sure that the ruler's ¼″ is accurate. (Many rulers are not printed with exact measures!) A steel draftsman's ruler is preferable to an acrylic rotary ruler for this purpose.

Once you have selected a presser foot for your machine (see Class 110, page 7), you will want to find a seam guide that works with that foot to help you sew straight and accurate seams and create accurate sewn units.

CHOOSING A SEAM GUIDE

You have several options, from simple, homemade guides to manufactured ones. These guides will provide a barrier for the edge of the fabric to glide against.

Masking tape. Harriet's students have great success using layers of ¼″ masking tape, available at quilt stores. A ⅛″-thick section of tape 2″ long secured to the throat plate and bed of your machine will create an excellent barrier guide to run the fabric edge against. (Make deep cuts into the roll of tape, and peel off a thick section between the cuts.) Place the tape in front of the right toe of the foot, especially if the foot is too wide for the seam allowance you need to use.

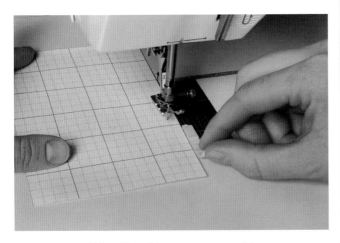

Using ¼″ masking tape as seam guide

Straight-stitch foot. Harriet's favorite foot, the Bernina #13 straight-stitch foot (see Class 110, page 7), has a guide bar that attaches to the foot. It makes sewing perfect seams easy, once you have positioned it accurately. After the guide bar is in position, the extra arm of the guide bar that extends to the left can be cut off to about ¾″.

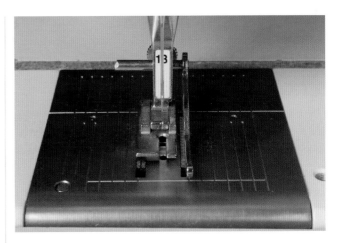

Bernina seam guide sits on top of right feed dog.

Mole foam. This adhesive padding, made to protect pressure points on people's feet, is also a commonly used seam guide. Use a ruler and a rotary cutter with an old blade inserted to cut the foam sheet into ¼″ × 2″ strips. Expose the adhesive, and position the strips on the bed of the machine. The only drawback to mole foam is that a groove will wear into the side over time. Keep an eye on this, and replace the foam as necessary, or your piecing can become inaccurate.

Other guides. Two-piece guides that screw into the bed of the machine have long been available. They are very accurate, and vibration from the machine never moves them out of place. Magnetic guides are available from various manufacturers, but they have drawbacks. Vibration can move them slightly, and they won't work on a machine with a plastic bed unless there is a large metal throat-plate area. If you have a computerized machine, check with your dealer to make sure this kind of guide can be used.

Various seam guides

LESSON THREE:
Sewing for accuracy

STITCH LENGTH

Once you have chosen a foot and placed a seam guide on your machine, you will need to set the machine to a stitch length that will give you a secure seam but will be long enough to rip out if necessary. It is important that you understand a little about stitch length and know the minimum, average, and maximum stitch length your machine can produce.

Your machine measures stitch length in either millimeters or stitches per inch. Most of the newer machines have stitch lengths measured in millimeters. Here is a basic guideline for what your machine is telling you if it measures in millimeters: 6 millimeters equals about ¼", so if you have the stitch length set at 6, your stitches will be about ¼" long. Another way to think about it is that if your machine is set at 2, then the stitches will measure 2mm long, and if we know that 6mm equals about ¼", then 2mm stitches are about ¹⁄₁₂", or 12 stitches to the inch.

The chart below shows you how these two measurements compare.

Stitches per inch	Millimeters (mm)
50	.5
25	1
16	1.5
12	2
10	2.5

We recommend that you set the stitch length between 12 and 14 stitches per inch, or 1.75 to 2 on a machine measuring in millimeters. This length will yield a secure seam and will allow you to slip a seam-ripper blade easily under a single stitch if you need to rip out a seam. Sew a couple of seams to see which stitch length you prefer.

✳ EXERCISE:
TESTING YOUR SEAM ALLOWANCE

Materials:

⅛ yard dark cotton fabric

⅛ yard light cotton fabric

Now you're ready to sew a test sample to check for accuracy. As you do this exercise, use the techniques you learned in Class 120, Lessons Three through Five. Select a dark fabric and a light fabric for contrast, and make sure that they both have the same thread count. Straighten the grain before cutting.

> *note* Here and throughout this book, we suggest that you read through the complete class before starting any exercises or projects, so that you understand all the steps before you actually perform them.

1. Cut a strip 2" wide from each fabric. Cut each strip into 7"-long pieces.

2. At the machine, place 2 strips right sides together with right edges aligned exactly.

3. Begin stitching at the end of the strips. (It is not necessary to backstitch at the beginning or end of seams, because intersecting seams at many points in the quilt will eventually hold those ends in place.) To keep the thread from getting jammed, hold the top and bottom threads together in your left hand as you begin to stitch.

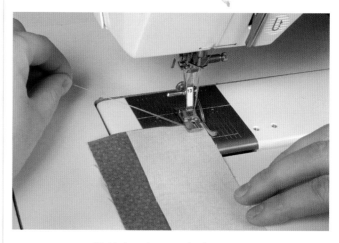

Hold threads as you begin to sew.

You may want to start with a small fabric scrap. Stitch on the scrap first, then feed in the strips. End the seam with a small scrap, too. Clip the scraps off the ends of the strips when you've finished sewing the seam.

Sewing on scrap to keep thread in order

4. Start stitching slowly to give the feed dogs a chance to grab the fabric. Let the machine do all the feeding. Avoid pushing or pulling at the fabric, as uneven, puckered seams can result. If you are new to sewing, run the machine at a fairly slow speed so that you have control in guiding the fabric. Keep your eye on the right edge of the fabric as it glides alongside the seam guide. There is no need to watch the presser foot or the needle.

5. When you've finished stitching, cut the thread tails *even* with the ends of the strips. Because you are just starting the learning process and we want to instill in you good habits, we want to stress how important this is. Do not use the thread cutter on your machine, and do not leave little tails, even ¼", dangling on the ends of your strips. This makes for very messy quilt backs and will add to your work when the quilt top is finished, because those little threads can get caught in other seams and show on the front. So please, start now and train yourself to trim the thread tails right down to the end of the fabric.

6. Press (see Lesson Four, page 26). Stitch a third strip to the first 2 so that you have a light-dark-light or dark-light-dark combination, trim the threads, and press again.

Here is where you will see the importance of an accurately sewn unit, and how you must work back from the finished sewn unit and adjust your seam allowance in order to end up with an accurate-sized unit. The finished unit should measure 5" wide. More importantly, the center strip should be a perfect 1½" wide. If you don't get these measurements, adjust your seam guide. If the center strip is narrower than 1½", the seam allowance was sewn too wide, and you must

position the seam guide closer to the needle. If the center strip is wider than 1½", the seam allowance was sewn too narrow, and you must position the seam guide farther away from the needle. You may have to place the seam guide in front of the toe of the foot instead of to the side in order to get it in the correct position.

Repeat the test with new strips to make an accurate finished unit.

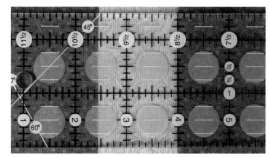

Seam allowance too narrow

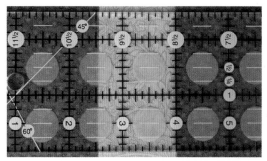

Seam allowance too wide

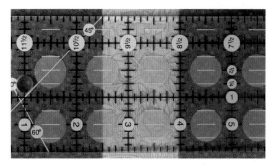

Seam allowance exactly right

note If the ¼" presser foot for your machine has a built-in guide on the side, you are probably taking a full ¼" seam allowance. Using Presencia 60/3 sewing thread will often allow you to sew accurately with this foot. If your foot is adjustable or slightly narrower than ¼", you can probably use a 50/3 thread and get a perfect finished unit. Test to see which thread weight works best for your machine and foot choice.

LESSON FOUR:
Pressing for success

If you iron your patchwork pieces with the vigorous approach that you use for a shirt, your quilt could be in trouble. Incorrect pressing can stretch, distort, and heat set the pieces into a real mess. However, if done correctly, pressing can truly enhance your piecework.

For most of the quilts in this book, you will press the seam allowances to one side. You will be pressing every seam (or, when chain piecing, a series of seams) as it is sewn instead of sewing several units and *then* trying to press accurately.

When you take two sewn pieces to the ironing board, consider the direction in which you're planning to press the seam allowance. Normally we press the seam allowance toward the darker fabric. Experience (or a sample block) will tell you whether or not this will work in a particular situation. To help you become familiar with the system, we provide a pressing plan for each of the quilts in this book.

When you are pressing, spray starch will become your best friend. It gives the fabric a crispness that makes it stay in place and track straight through the machine—no stretching or distortion. The finished block will be very straight and square and have a crisp, firm finish.

✳ EXERCISE: PRESSING A SEAM

Materials:

> Sample from Exercise: Testing your seam allowance (page 25)
>
> Iron
>
> Faultless Heavy spray starch

1. Place the sewn pieces on the ironing board with the seam allowance away from you and whichever piece of fabric the seam allowances will be directed toward on top. Using steam, press in the closed position first to set the stitches. Steam softens the fabric, helps it bend more easily, and aids in preventing stretching and distortion.

Setting seam in closed position

2. Lift up the top strip and glide the iron gently up against and over the seam allowance. If you set the iron down on top of the opened pieces without first directing the seam allowance, you run the risk of pressing in glitches, pleats, and puckers. Use the iron's side edge, not the point. Here, a heavy iron is to your advantage because its weight does the work for you. Do not pull on the strip with your fingers. Use *only* the pressure on the iron.

Pushing seam allowance to side

> **tip** Remember to always press from the right side of the fabric.

3. Once the seam has been pressed over, apply a *very light* misting of spray starch to the seam. (If the fabric appears wet, you are using too much starch!) Turn the steam off, and press the starch dry. Each time you press, you are applying light pressure and pushing against the seam with the side of the iron.

4. Apply up to 3 *light* layers of starch. The starch will give the seam a very sharp, flat edge, which will keep the piecing accurate each step of the way. As each seam is added to the unit, this process is repeated before you proceed to the next step.

> **tip** If you press a seam allowance in the wrong direction, don't just flip it the other way and run the iron over it. Fold the two pieces together again, and reset the seam closed; then open it, and re-press in the opposite direction.

LESSON FIVE: Let's sew!

Now you are ready to construct your first patchwork! You'll start by making the center quilt block for Carrie's sampler quilt. As you make the sample units in the exercises, they will eventually be put together into a small quilt that you will complete in Volume 2 of this series. This is a perfect way to learn the techniques in this book, because it allows you to try each technique and get it right before starting on the larger projects assigned at the end of each class.

Sampler quilt that you will construct during practice sessions

❋ EXERCISE: SAMPLER QUILT BLOCKS

Materials:

½ yard solid blue fabric (Fabric A, dark)

½ yard blue print fabric (Fabric B, light)

½ yard white background fabric (Note: This will be used in Volume 2 when you learn diagonal settings for the Nine-Patch blocks made later in this book.)

The blocks you will construct are made in a pattern called Fence Post. As you complete this exercise, please keep in mind these objectives:

❋ Cut extremely accurate strips.

❋ Watch carefully that all raw edges are exactly and constantly aligned with each other.

❋ Sew exact, straight seams.

❋ Double-check your cutting and sewing by remeasuring the strips after pressing and trimming off threads.

CONSTRUCTING STRIP SETS

1. Tear the ends of the fabrics and straighten the grain as described in Class 120, page 16).

2. Cut 3 strips 2″ wide from each of the A and B fabrics as described in Class 120.

3. You will be sewing these into strip sets. One set will be dark-light-dark, and the other set will be light-dark-light.

Strip set combinations

4. Align a Fabric A strip and a Fabric B strip right sides together, making sure that the raw edges are EXACTLY aligned. (If the edges are not aligned, the strips won't be the correct width after sewing, and the accuracy of the entire unit will be off.) Stitch them together. Repeat with another set of strips. This is the beginning of both strip sets. Remember—when you take the sewn strips off the machine, trim those threads down to the fabric!

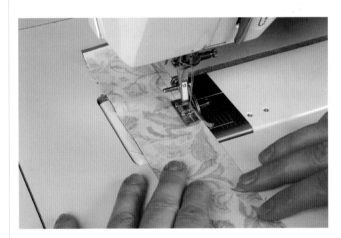

Perfectly aligned edges

Always trim threads close.

5. Press both strip sets as described in Exercise: Pressing a seam (page 26). The seam allowances should be pressed toward the darkest fabric. As you press, make sure the strips stay arrow straight. Avoid letting them bend into an arc. Lightly starch, misting and pressing with a dry iron up to 3 times until the seam is perfectly straight and flat.

6. Lay the pressed strip sets on the cutting mat, and, with a ruler, check to see that they are both exactly 1¾″ wide. If they are a tiny bit wider, trim off any extra fabric to make each strip exactly 1¾″ wide. If they are narrower, check to see whether the seams are both pressed and sewn straight, and double-check the seam guide placement. Pressing is often the biggest problem in piecing. If you can pull on the seam and it gives at all, it is not pressed properly.

Ruler placement to check strip width

> *hint* For easy ripping when a seam needs to be done over, use a seam ripper to cut every third stitch on one side and unravel the thread from the opposite side.

7. You are now ready to add the third strip to each strip set, making a dark-light-dark and a light-dark-light combination. Sew, press, starch, and measure as above. This strip should also be exactly 1¾″ wide. After the third strip has been added, check that your seam allowance is still accurate by measuring the center strip and making sure it is 1½″ along the entire length of the strip.

Each strip set should measure 5″ wide down the entire length of the strips. If there is a waver anywhere along the length, cut out and discard that portion, or rip out and resew.

Now you're ready to cut the strip sets into segments.

LESSON SIX: Cutting segments accurately

Check your work from the last lesson. After you have sewn the three strips together and trimmed the edges even, the width of the three strips (strip set) should be exact along the entire length of the strip set. If it is not, consider these questions:

✳ Were the strips cut accurately?

✳ Were the edges of the strips aligned exactly when you were stitching?

✳ Are all the seams sewn straight and accurately? Cutting the strip sets into segments accurately in the next steps is very important. The seams will be what you measure from, not just the raw edge.

✳ Have you pressed any folds into the seams that caused the strip sets to be uneven?

Make sure the strip sets are accurate before continuing. Remember, this is the key to making accurate blocks.

CUTTING SEGMENTS

1. Place a strip set on the cutting mat, and lay a ruler across the strips. Align the cross lines of the ruler evenly with the sewn seams. This will tell you whether the strips are perfectly straight and all the same width. Trim the end off the strip set, wasting as little fabric as possible but removing the selvages completely.

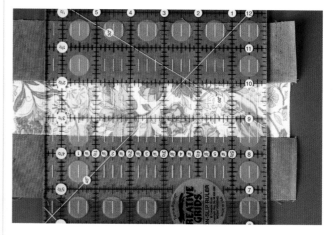

Trimming the end using proper ruler alignment

2. Turn the strip 180°, so that the length of the strip is on the same side as the hand you cut with. Next, align the measurement needed with the cut edge. The strip sets are 5″ wide, so you will cut segments 5″ long. Be sure the 5″ ruler line is exactly aligned with the cut edge of the fabric, and the perpendicular ruler lines are exactly aligned with the seamlines. Cut 5 segments 5″ long of the dark-light-dark strip set and 4 segments 5″ long from the light-dark-light strip set.

> *note* Cut only one strip set at a time. Many quilt project instructions tell you to stack the sets and cut multiples, but the chance of inaccurate cuts is very high. Cut two to three segments as instructed and realign the edge if it is getting out of square. The cut edge and the perpendicular seams must always stay in alignment.

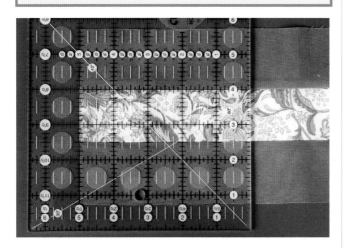

You are now ready to lay out the blocks to form the center section of the sampler quilt. This is a perfect time to learn how to chain piece and how to butt seams.

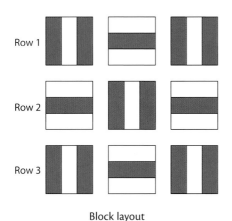

Block layout

CHAIN PIECING

Chain piecing is a quick and efficient way to stitch identical units together. You feed and stitch the units one after the other, without lifting the presser foot or cutting the thread in between. To begin, lay out the blocks as shown in the photo on page 27. You now need to pick them up in the correct order to get them to your sewing machine. Here's a foolproof way to do it.

1. Starting with Row 1, pick up the first block on the left, lay it on top of the second block, and lay those on top of the third block. Pin the pile together at the top of the block to remind you which way is "up," and lay the stack back down. This stack is Row 1. Repeat with the second and third rows. You now have 3 stacks with 3 blocks in each, with the first block of each row on top of each stack. Place the Row 1 stack on top of Row 2, and place those stacks on top of Row 3.

Stacking up rows

2. Take the stacks to the machine. Lay them out in order to the right of the machine. Select something like a paperweight, a bobbin, or a small pair of scissors to use as a marker. Unpin the stacks, and place the marker on top of Row 1.

3. Immediately move the marker to Row 2, and pick up the first block from Row 1 in your left hand and the second block from Row 1 in your right hand. Place the second block on top of the first, right sides together, and stitch together the right-hand edge.

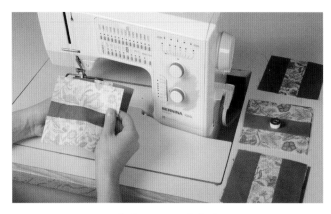

Block 2 on top of Block 1

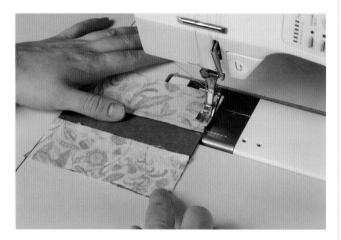

Sewing the right edge

4. When you come to the end of the seam, stop. *Do not cut the thread.* You will be chain sewing another set of blocks onto this set.

5. Move the marker from Row 2 to Row 3. Pick up the first and second blocks from Row 2, and stitch as in Step 3, leaving about ¼″ of thread between the blocks for Row 1 and Row 2.

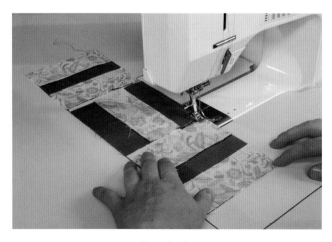

Chain feeding

6. Stop at the end of the seam. Move the marker back to Row 1, pick up the first 2 blocks of Row 3, stitch as in Step 3, and cut the threads. Now the first 2 blocks from each row are stitched to each other and chained together in the order of the rows.

7. Press all the seams. (You do not need to cut the rows apart, but you can if you feel it is necessary. If you do cut them apart, be sure to keep the rows in order.) Press each seam closed first. Next, if you do not cut the rows apart, let Rows 2 and 3 hang off the edge of the ironing board while you press the seam for Row 1 to the left, working from the right side of the fabric. Pull up Row 2, and, working on the edge of the ironing board, press this seam to the right, from the right side. Finally, bring up Row 3, and press again to the left, just like Row 1. You are pressing the seams toward the vertical strip so that the seam allowances are not pressed back on top of themselves.

Pressing seams of each row

8. Now sew the third and last block from each stack to its row. Pick up the last block from Stack 1 and stitch it to the second block of Row 1, right sides together, along the right edge. Next comes Row 2, still attached to Row 1. Stitch the last block of Row 2 onto the second block. Repeat for the last block on Row 3.

Adding Block 3

9. You are now out of blocks, and all 3 rows have been constructed. When the rows are complete, you might find it helpful to separate them by cutting the chain threads, but you can keep them attached. Press the seams toward the vertical strips at every seam. Press from the right side.

> *tip* This stacking method can be used for any size quilt. Once you work out the system, you will find that it is fast and efficient, and you can check the pattern layout as you go. It eliminates all the getting up and down needed to pick up a few blocks at a time.

BUTTING SEAMS

As you prepare to sew rows together, you will need to butt the seams, meaning that you will nest them together (but not on top of each other) so they lie flat. The ability to butt seams successfully is very dependent on the accuracy of your cutting and sewing. If you are trying to join units that are different sizes, it will be difficult to get anything to fit and stay in position.

Place Row 1 on top of Row 2. Using your fingers, bring the seam allowances together, aligning the seams. Because you have pressed the seam allowances in opposite directions, the seam ridges will "butt" together. This is something you feel with your fingers. If there is a bump in the middle of the seam, the seam allowances are probably on top of one another, and the seams are not aligned properly. If there is a "valley" or spread between the seams, they are too far apart. When the area feels flat and even, the seams are interlocked and ready to sew.

Seams perfectly nested or butted

You will find that as you gain experience, you will be able to hold the seams in place and stitch right up to your fingers, and the seams will butt perfectly. Butting seams accurately is critical to good piecing as well as to successfully quilting the top later.

SUCCESSFUL PINNING

In the beginning, you may feel the need to pin these seams together to keep them from shifting when you are stitching. If so, use the finest pins available. The thicker the pin, the more distortion will occur when the pin is inserted into the seam allowance. Following are three pinning methods.

❊ With seam allowances aligned, place a pin on each side of the stitching so the pinheads extend beyond the fabric edge. Remove them, one at a time, just before you stitch over them.

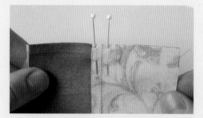

Pinning on both sides of seam

❊ Place the pin *parallel* to the fabric edge on the stitching line. Remove the pin as the needle approaches it.

Pinning through the seam allowance, parallel to edge

❊ If you are using *very* fine pins, such as Clover Patchwork Pins, you can pin with the heads inside the body of the block and the points along the fabric edge, and simply sew over the points. If you are using a barrier-type seam guide such as tape, mole foam, or a screw-on or magnetic seam guide, you do not need to remove the pins when you come to them.

Pin points at edge

SEWING TOGETHER THE ROWS

1. Hold or pin Row 1 to Row 2, and stitch the rows together.

2. Press the seam allowance to set it, and then press it toward Row 1. (Let Row 3 hang off the front edge of the ironing board.) Stand Row 1 up, and, with the edge of the iron, carefully push Row 1 over to lie flat on the ironing board. Gently work the seam with the edge of the iron until it is flat and perfect. You will be going over the lumps of the seam allowances, so work carefully to keep from distorting the seam.

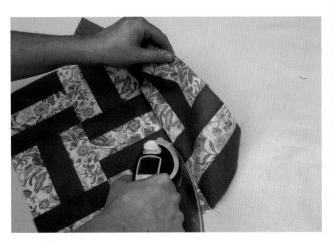

Stand Row 1 up.

3. Stitch Row 3 to Row 2, butting each seam exactly. Direct the seam toward Row 2, and press, following the same steps as above.

Now you have a square patchwork piece made up of three rows of three blocks each. This small piece should measure 14″ × 14″ from raw edge to raw edge in both directions. Check for squareness, flatness, and dimension. Check that all the seams are butted exactly.

Congratulations! You have completed your first piece of patchwork. You will use these methods and techniques throughout this book and all the books in the series, so if you are having any problems with accuracy now, go back and repeat the steps until you work out where the problems are. We can't stress accuracy enough! If your work starts out with problems, the piece will only get worse as you continue. It is so much easier to get it right every step of the way.

Next, you get to put your new skills to use to construct a simple quilt.

LESSON SEVEN:
Your first quilts

For your first two projects, we present a choice of two small quilts that are basic in design and simple to make. You might be tempted to jump ahead to more flashy designs, but please take the time to make one of these basic quilts so that you can start at the beginning and develop your skills as you go. With precise cutting, sewing, and ironing, you will have a wonderful experience on your first try. We offer you two options: Harriet's *Woodland Winter* and Carrie's *Cowboy Corral*. Both feature Fence Post blocks and fun prints used in different ways.

> **note** In these and subsequent quilt projects, we will explain how to figure out the number of strips you need to cut and sew. This will gently lead you into learning how to figure yardage, which will be taught in detail in Class 170. Right now, the basic information you need is the answers to the following questions:
>
> *How many blocks are needed for the quilt?*
>
> *How many inches does each block require from each strip set?*
>
> *How many strip sets does it take to accommodate that many blocks?*
>
> We have always figured on fabric being 42″ wide, once the selvages have been removed. Other books set the standard at 40″. We suggest that you measure the width of your fabrics before cutting, and rework our figures to fit your needs. If your fabrics all give you 42″ or more of length per strip, you might not need to sew that extra strip set. However, if your fabrics are running short, you will be glad that you don't have to go back and cut strips for one more set. It is well worth your time to do the math first!

PROJECT: HARRIET'S *WOODLAND WINTER* QUILT

Woodland Winter is a small children's quilt that uses a single set of strips and a fun print border. The strips are of a predetermined width, and the plain squares are cut the size of the finished Fence Post blocks.

Quilt top size: 33" × 33" (without border)

Grid size of strip: 1" (1½" cut)

Block size: 3" × 3"

Blocks:

60 pieced Fence Post blocks

49 blue squares

12 white print squares

Layout: 11 rows of 11 blocks each

Yardages for quilt top:

¾ yard blue fabric

⅜ yard red fabric

⅓ yard white print fabric

1¼ yards border stripe if fabric has 4 repeats across the width, dependent on the width of the stripe (Read Class 180 before purchasing a border stripe.)

Study the photo of the quilt and identify the different units needed for this project. You will see that only one set of strips is needed to make the Fence Post blocks. The strip set is made up of blue, red, and white fabrics. The pattern is developed by turning the pieced blocks differently in each row. Each pieced block is next to a plain block.

Woodland Winter

Before you begin, be sure to straighten your yardage as described in Class 120, Lesson Three.

Units needed for quilt

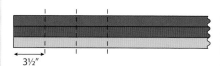

3½"

The strip set needed

MAKING THE FENCE POST BLOCKS

1. Determine how many strips you must cut. There are 60 blocks. If the fabric is cut on the crosswise grain, you have 42" of usable fabric (see Note, page 32). The grid is 1",

meaning you will cut the strips 1½" wide. These strips will be sewn into strip sets, which will be cut into 3½" × 3½" units. Divide the strip length (fabric width—42") by the strip set width (3½") to get 12 units from 1 set of strips. We need 60 blocks, so divide 60 by 12 to get your answer—5 strip sets.

> *note* Measure the width of your fabric. If you have 40 usable inches, you will get 11 blocks 3½" × 3½" per strip set. To make 60 blocks, you need six strip sets, but you may use little of the sixth one. This is why it is important to know how wide your fabric is—you may need to make an extra set if your fabric is unusually narrow.

2. Cut 5 strips 1½″ wide from each of the 3 fabrics you've chosen for the Fence Post blocks of your quilt. Lay each color in stacks, and lay the stacks beside your machine in the order they will be sewn: blue-red-white (see Chain piecing, page 30). Working from left to right with the strip stacks, stitch all the blue and red strips right sides together, placing a red strip on top of a blue strip.

Layout of stacks and strip orientation

3. Press the seams to one side, starching as you go. Remember to measure the width of each strip to make sure each strip is now exactly 1¼″ wide. If the strips are too narrow, check your sewing and pressing, and resew if necessary. If they are a bit too wide, trim them. Next, sew the white strip to the red strip, and repeat for all 5 sets. Refer to the photo on page 33 for guidance.

Adding last strip

4. Press and starch again, directing the seam allowance as for the first seams (Step 3).

note Check your work once more. The strips should be straight. The outer strips should measure exactly 1¼″ wide, and the center strip exactly 1″ wide for the entire length of the strip set. If there is a problem, check your seam guide to make sure you are sewing the correct seam allowance. Also check the following:

Were the strips cut exactly 1½″ wide?

Are the seams sewn perfectly straight?

Has pressing caused stretching or pleats?

Correct any problems before going on to the next step.

5. To cut the strip sets into segments, lay a ruler on top of the strip set and align the ruler lines with the seams, not the raw edges. Trim off the end to create a straight and square edge. Refer to the photo in Cutting segments (page 28) for guidance.

6. Turn the strip 180° and lay the 3½″ ruler line on the edge you just cut. Align the ruler lines again with the seams and cut. You now have a 3½″ × 3½″ square. Continue cutting all 5 strip sets to make 60 Fence Post blocks. Refer to the photo in Cutting segments (page 29) for guidance.

Measure from raw edge and seamlines.

MAKING THE PLAIN SQUARES

1. From the blue fabric, cut 5 strips 3½″ wide. Cut those strips into 3½″ × 3½″ squares. You will need 49 blue squares.

2. From the white print fabric, cut 1 strip 3½″ wide. Cut the strip into 12 squares 3½″ × 3½″.

ASSEMBLING THE QUILT TOP

1. Lay out the squares and Fence Post blocks, using the illustration below as a guide. Row 1 uses only the blue squares, and the Fence Post blocks are turned 180° in every other position, with their seams running horizontally. Row 2 uses both the white print and blue squares, with the Fence Post blocks again turned 180° each time, but now the seams are vertical instead of horizontal.

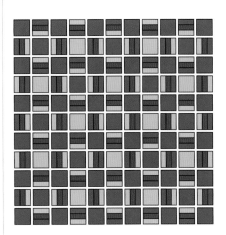

Block layout

2. With all the blocks and squares positioned, start in the top left corner and stack Block 1 on top of Block 2, on top of Block 3, and so forth, until all the Row 1 blocks (working left to right) are in 1 stack. Pin the stack together at the *top* of the block to remind you which way is "up." Repeat for the remaining rows, making sure the rows are in order, with Block 1 from each row on top.

3. Place the stacks to the right of your machine, laying them out in rows, and in order.

Blocks laid beside machine in sewing order

4. Remove the pins from the stacks. Using the technique you learned for chain piecing, page 29), begin sewing the rows together. Place Block 2 from Row 1 (Stack 1) on top of Block 1, right sides together, and stitch together the right edges of the blocks. Repeat with Row 2 (Stack 2), and follow through until the first 2 blocks of all 11 rows have been chain stitched together.

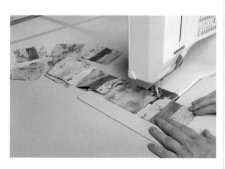

Sewing first two blocks of all rows together

5. Do not cut the threads between the blocks. Press the seam allowances toward the solid blocks.

6. Next, sew the top block of Row 1 (Block 3) to the first pair of the chain, right sides together. Similarly, sew the top block of Row 2 to the next pair of the chain. Continue until the remaining top blocks have been added to all the rows. Press the seams toward the solid blocks.

Adding third block to all rows

7. Continue adding blocks to each row until all 11 blocks have been sewn together. Press after each addition.

All blocks have been added to every row.

Let rows hang off edge of ironing board when pressing seam.

8. Because every other block is a solid square, and all the seam allowances are pressed toward a solid square, the seams should easily align to butt together. Lay Row 1 on top of Row 2, right sides together, and align seams, pinning if necessary. Stitch.

9. Press the seam toward Row 1. To make it easy to press one row at a time, place only Rows 1 and 2 on top of the ironing board and let the rest of the rows hang off the edge. Starch once the seam allowance has been pressed, and continue to sew the rows together, pressing each row as you go.

---

border information for this quilt

The border for this quilt is a printed border stripe that has multiple small stripes in it. This border stripe finishes to be 5½" wide.

Congratulations! You have finished your first quilt top. We hope you have a fun border print picked out to frame this little quilt. Adding borders will be taught in Class 180, so lay aside your new creation for now, and let's move on to another project!

PROJECT: CARRIE'S *COWBOY CORRAL* QUILT

This quilt uses a fabric featuring small square panels printed with cowboy motifs. If you use a fun fabric with pictures that can be cut into squares, those squares will determine the size of the strips, as well as how many units you need in order to make a quilt the size you want. You will need to *fussy cut* the squares, as described on page 37.

Quilt top size: 40½″ × 49½″ (without borders)

Grid size of strip: 1½″ (2″ cut)

Block size: 4½″ × 4½″

Blocks:

　50 panel squares

　49 Fence Post blocks

Layout: 11 rows of 9 blocks each

Yardages for quilt top:

　Panel print or large-print fabric (see below) for the squares

　For the Fence Post blocks:

　　½ yard blue fabric

　　½ yard green fabric

　　½ yard gold fabric

　　¼ yard red fabric for border

　　⅞ yard brown fabric for border

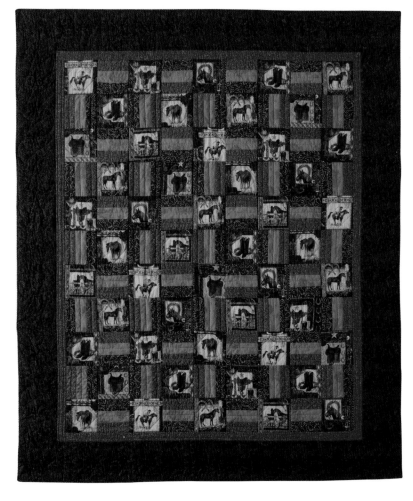

Cowboy Corral

MAKING THE QUILT

The layout and construction for this quilt top are the same as for *Woodland Winter* (page 33).

First cut out the panel squares. Next, cut strips from the blue, green, and gold fabrics to make the Fence Post blocks.

Make 7 strip sets of the blue-gold-green combination. How did we get this number? The finished panel square is 4½″ × 4½″ (5″ × 5″ cut). The strips are cut 2″ wide and finish at 1½″ wide. Three strips are sewn together, so 1½″ × 3 = 4½″ + ½″ seam allowance = strip set width. Each strip set is 42″ long and 5″ wide with seam allowances. The quilt calls for 49 Fence Post blocks. Each strip set yields 8 units. 49 ÷ 8 = 6.125, which is rounded up to 7 strip sets needed. 7 strips × 2″ cut = 14″ fabric needed. This would be ½ yard of each, including a 4″ margin for error.

Once you have the Fence Post blocks assembled, follow the steps for *Woodland Winter* to complete the quilt top.

border information for this quilt

The small inner border for this quilt is cut from the red fabric and finishes to be 1¼″ wide. The outer border is brown and is 5¾″ wide, finished.

Have fun!

Quilt patterns such as *Cowboy Corral* give you a great opportunity to use fabrics that have large prints or fun motifs. To target and cut out a certain element or motif, you will do what quilters call *fussy cutting*. This requires more fabric than you would need if you were just cutting strips for pieced blocks, as for *Woodland Winter*. If you're not sure at the time you buy the fabric how big your quilt is going to be or what quilt pattern you are going to make, buy at least twice the amount you would normally need.

If you're buying fabric to make a specific quilt, count how many motifs you can cut from a yard, and figure how many you need. In *Cowboy Corral*, the motifs are used in every solid square, so you need 50 motif panels. But you could create a secondary design with the motif fabric and use a second fabric for the alternating solid squares, thus reducing the yardage you would need. Be sure to allow for the space needed for a seam allowance around the picture. This often cuts into a neighboring picture, reducing the number of usable motifs you can get from the yardage.

There are several rulers and tools on the market that can help you cut the panels. A ruler made by Creative Grid lets you lay the ruler over the area you want to cut, mark the corners of the square as registration marks, and then use a smaller ruler to align those marks and cut out the square. Many ruler companies offer square rulers in different sizes. Smaller sizes such as 2", 2½", 3", 3½", 4", or 4½" square will help you cut out those squares easily and accurately.

First iron and starch the fabric well. Don't worry about straightening the fabric; large printed designs are rarely perfectly on-grain. Starching the fabric well will help counteract problems with fabric that is a little off-grain.

Lay out the fabric on your cutting surface in a single layer. Place a square ruler over the design you wish to capture, and, if you are using a ruler that is exactly the size of the square, cut carefully around all 4 sides of the ruler. If you are using a larger ruler, cut the side and the top of the square, then turn the ruler and align the edges you just cut with the lines on the ruler that correspond to the size of the square you are cutting. Now cut the other 2 sides of the square.

Make sure that you are cutting a measurement that is divisible by 3. Because you will sew together 3 strips for the Fence Post blocks, which have to equal the size of the panel, you want quilter-friendly numbers. Cutting ⅛" increments can be tricky for a beginner, so if you can work with ¼" increments it makes the cutting easier.

❋ 3½" cut panel square = 1½" cut strips for Fence Post block (1" grid, 3" finished panel square)
❋ 4¼" cut panel square = 1¾" cut strips (1¼" grid, 3¾" finished panel square)
❋ 5" cut panel square = 2" cut strips (1½" grid, 4½" finished panel square)

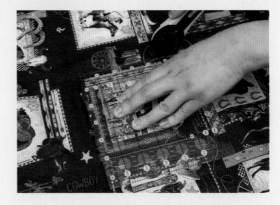

Cutting with larger ruler

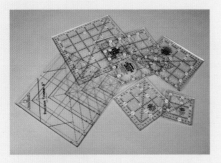

Rulers to help with fussy cutting

Class 140

LESSON ONE:
Upgrading your sewing area

Now that you have made a quilt top, you might be ready to make some changes in where and how your machine is set up, your ironing work-station, and your cutting surface. This class will provide more in-depth information about setting up a good work area. Then we will venture into making slightly more challenging quilts.

SEWING TABLES

Your table and chair are critical to a comfortable work session. When starting out, you seldom have the perfect sewing cabinet, the right ergo-nomic chair, and the perfect light. But you can make do with whatever you have available, as long as you observe some basic ergonomic principles.

The standard height of a sewing machine cabinet is 28″–32″. If your machine were in a cabinet, that would be the height of the machine bed. If you will be working with your machine on a table, try to use a table low enough that the bed of the machine is within this range. You can buy an adjustable-height banquet table (avoid the plastic ones, which vibrate too much) and set it at the right height for sewing. These tables are a good investment because you can always adjust them when you need a higher table for a different task.

Special portable tables, such as the SewEzi (pictured), are also available. These are very stable, and they take up little space. Other brands are made by Roberts and Sew Much More.

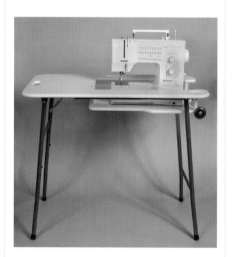

SewEzi portable table

Your machine should be close enough to you that you are not stretching your arms or your neck to see the needle. The needle should not be more than 7″ from the edge of the table. The proper body position for sitting at the sewing machine is very similar to that for playing the piano.

Make sure you can sit directly in front of the needle, not in front of the machine. You also need enough leg-room to be comfortable, and you should be able to pull your chair close enough to work comfortably for several hours.

The chair you choose to sit on while sewing can make the difference between a pleasant sewing session and backaches. It must be comfortable and provide firm support.

Sitting at a sewing machine is much like working at a computer keyboard. When everything is adjusted correctly as shown below, your elbows are at the same height as the keyboard. The line from your elbow to your hand is straight or has only a slight downward tilt of the wrist (a 90° angle, plus or minus 20°). Following these guidelines can nearly eliminate wrist stress when sewing. Try it and see.

Sitting at your machine pain-free

LIGHTING

We would suggest that you invest in a good task light to position by your machine. Full-spectrum, true-color lighting eliminates glare and eye fatigue. We recommend Ott and Daylight lamps, which come in many sizes and styles. A lamp on a flex arm that can be positioned at any angle is very convenient.

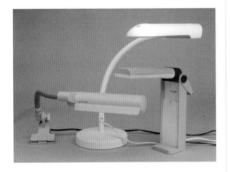

Selection of good lamps for sewing

LESSON TWO:
Cutting and ironing area refinements

CUTTING TABLE ERGONOMICS

A cutting table is one of the most important working areas of a sewing room. We spend as much if not more time at the cutting table than we do at the sewing machine. Designing, planning, cutting, and developing projects often takes place at the cutting table. This table needs to be customized to your height and space requirements. The ideal table should be accessible from all four sides, hard-surfaced, and high enough so you don't have to stoop or bend while working.

The ideal size is determined by the types of projects you undertake. Generally, a table 28″ to 36″ wide and 56″ to 72″ long is sufficient for quilting. Your work should be kept to within 14″ to 18″ of your body on the table surface. Reaching too far can hurt your back and reduce your muscle power. The center of the table width should be between 14″ and 18″ from the edge.

To determine the table's proper height, stand in the shoes you normally work in, bend your elbow at a 90° angle, measure from the elbow to the floor, and subtract 2″ to 3″. Ideally, you should be able to perform the task without raising your hand above elbow level and without stooping or stretching forward.

Place a rubber or padded mat on the floor in front of the table to reduce circulation problems and fatigue from standing for long periods.

Ideas for making a table work for you include the following:

❋ If you are using a folding banquet-type table, raise the height either by extending the legs with precut lengths of metal or PVC pipe (a diameter that will just slip over the legs) or by placing wood blocks measuring 4″ × 4″ × the needed height under each leg. Nail a small can on each block of wood to keep the legs in place. Bed risers also work if they provide a height that is right for you.

❋ A real space saver is a door fastened to the wall at one end and supported on the other end by a dresser or pre-made kitchen cabinet base unit. Or use a door with dressers or cabinet bases for the supports at both ends.

❋ Create a reversible tabletop with one side laminated for cutting and the other side padded for pressing large pieces.

IRON

As you get started, you will likely make do with the iron that you already own. As you progress with your piecing, you will see where specific features really do make a difference in the way an iron performs.

If possible, use an iron with the least number of holes on the soleplate. The more holes, the more likely the fabric is to catch in them and get "scrunched up." More holes also mean less drying surface. Optimally, you need an iron with just a few holes at the very point of the iron so that when you use steam, the steam comes out of these holes and then is followed by a dry, flat surface that dries the fabric.

Iron with steam vents only at point

The heavier the iron, the easier it is for you to press accurately. Instead of your having to apply pressure to the iron, the weight of the iron does the work, and all you have to do is glide it over the surface.

Be sure to keep the soleplate of your iron clean. Dye, starch, and fabric finishes can build up on the iron, causing it to drag and to transfer residue onto seam allowances as you press. Try products such as Iron Off, which contain beeswax and silicone, to keep the iron clean and slick. You can also use white vinegar on a soft cloth to clean off the residue.

STARCH

This question comes up all the time: what is the difference between starch and sizing? You will often be told to use sizing instead of starch, but why? We were curious, so we called Faultless Starch Company in Kansas City to inquire (Faultless is our favorite band). Sizing is a product that gives washed garments that nice new feel that they had on the rack when you bought them. Starch actually stiffens the fabric and allows an iron to create a crease and hold it in the fabric. We prefer starch because when we press a seam, we want a crisp, sharp edge on the right side of the fabric, and for the fabric to lie very flat. This makes the piecing process go much easier and helps in many ways with the machine quilting process at the end.

Use starch when you straighten the grain and with every seam that you press. The accuracy that results makes it one of the most helpful things you can do to achieve perfect piecing.

LESSON THREE:
Useful gadgets

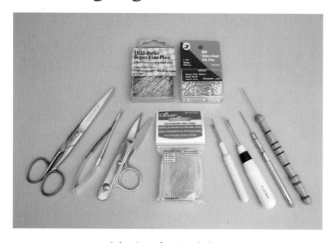

Selection of sewing helpers

SCISSORS

At this stage, you will not be cutting much fabric with scissors, but you will need thread scissors or snips. These are generally shorter and have more pointed tips than fabric scissors. Some brands are available with large holes for larger fingers. Thread snips are very handy for machine work. They are spring-loaded so that they are open all the time.

PINS

As you go through the piecing lessons, experiment to see if pins work for you. Experienced quilters tend to dislike pinning unless there is no other way to line pieces up. When it's possible to use alternating, butted seams and finger matching, many quilters feel they get a much more accurate join for the pieces. However, there is no way to join a long border strip to a quilt top accurately without using pins.

If you find you like using pins, the pins you choose can have a big effect on the piecing. Many pins sold as "quilter's" pins are too thick and create a bump at the seams. The extra-large head does not lie flat and can cause inaccurate stitching because the fabric is not allowed to lie flat against the throat plate of the machine.

We recommend using the finest pins you can find. Clover Patchwork Pins are the finest on the market. Others to try are IBC Fine Silk Pins by Clotilde, and Iris Silk Pins, in either the blue tin or the orange plaid box by Gingham Square.

We recommend that you do not sew over pins. Remove them as you come to them. The extra-fine Clover Patchwork Pins are an exception to this; still, slow down the machine a little just to make sure your needle clears the pin.

STILETTO

Some quilters use a tool to help guide the fabric under the presser foot, especially when they need to hold an area tight to make sure it doesn't slip as it passes under the presser foot. A stiletto is a very sharp metal point that works very well. You might want to consider an orange stick or bamboo skewer as an alternative.

SEAM RIPPER

In the beginning, your seam ripper will be your best friend. When shopping for a good seam ripper, there are a few things to consider. First, check your sewing machine attachment box. The very best seam ripper may come with your machine.

You are looking for the following characteristics:

* A very fine, sharp point to slip easily under a stitch
* A sharp cutting edge to cut the thread
* A comfortable handle, small or large—your preference

At this point, you're ready to move on to making quilts with more strips and colors.

LESSON FOUR:
The next step

In this lesson, you'll delve even further into quilts made with strips and only strips. The two quilts presented here differ greatly in construction techniques and will further your skills and abilities.

PROJECT: HARRIET'S *TRIPLE RAIL FENCE* QUILT

Quilt top size: 33¾″ × 41¼″ (without borders)

Grid size of strip: 1¼″ (1¾″ cut)

Block size: 3¾″ × 3¾″

Blocks:

50 blocks of Strip Set A

49 blocks of Strip Set B

Layout: 11 rows of 9 blocks each

Yardages for quilt top: **

¼ yard red fabric (Fabric 1)

¼ yard tan fabric (Fabric 2)

¼ yard green fabric (Fabric 3)

¼ yard light green print fabric (Fabric 4)

½ yard large-scale floral print fabric (Fabric 5)

⅛ yard red fabric for inner border

⅝ yard large-scale floral print fabric for outer border

Cut: *

6 strips 1¾″ wide of the red, tan, green, and light green print fabrics (Fabrics 1, 2, 3, and 4)

12 strips 1¾″ wide of the large-scale floral print fabric (Fabric 5)

*To determine how many strip sets you will need, the process is the same

Triple Rail Fence

as for *Woodland Winter* page 33). The blocks cut from the strip sets will measure 4¼″ × 4¼″. You will need 50 blocks of Strip Set A. Multiply 50 blocks × 4.25″ = 212.50″. Divide by 42″ (the fabric width): 212.50″ ÷ 42″ = 5.06. Rounding up, you need 6 of Strip Set A. You need 49 blocks of Strip Set B. So, 4.25″ × 49 blocks = 208.25″ ÷ 42″ = 4.96. You need 5 of Strip Set B.

**Each strip is cut 1¾″ wide. To determine yardage, figure 5 strips × 1.75″ = 8.75″. You need ¼ yard, or ⅓ yard including a margin for error. Each fabric is used once except for the large-scale print. It is used in both strip sets, so you will need twice as much of it.

Triple Rail Fence is very similar to the Fence Post quilts you made in Class 130, but there are more colors, two different strip sets, and a more complex layout.

The secret to a good *Triple Rail Fence* quilt is choosing a large-scale print fabric and four more fabrics that play well together. If you look at the photo closely, you will see that the placement of the fabrics develops the rails. The fabrics on the outsides of the strip sets will be the rails. These can be strong and really stand out, or they can blend into a wider, braided look.

One fabric (Fabric 5) will be every other rail in the quilt.

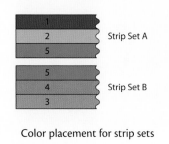
MAKING THE STRIP SETS

1. Sewing the strips together for this quilt is no different from sewing the strips for *Woodland Winter* (page 34). There are just more of them, and 2 color combinations. Lay out the strips beside your machine in this order: 1-2-5-4-3. There will be twice as many 5's, because they are used in both sets.

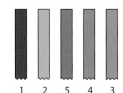

Strips laid out for sewing

2. Starting with the left stack of strips, place a #2 strip on top of a #1 strip and sew them together. Continue until all of stacks 1 and 2 are gone.

3. Press, starch, measure, and correct the strip width by trimming as necessary. Each strip should measure 1½″. Add the #5 strips to the #2 strips. Press, starch, and measure for accuracy. This is Strip Set A and should measure 4¼″ wide down the entire length of each strip set.

4. To construct Strip Set B, repeat the above process, adding #4 to #5, then #3 to #4. You now have 6 strip sets of each color combination.

5. Straighten the end of each strip set to establish a straight and square edge with the internal seams. Measure 4¼″ from this edge, using the seams and ruler lines to keep everything aligned.

ASSEMBLING THE QUILT TOP

1. You are now ready to lay out the blocks in the pattern. Using the following illustration and blocks from Strip Set B, start with 1 block with the seams vertical and then another of the same block with the seams horizontal. Repeat with Strip Set A. Repeat this pattern, alternating blocks from both strip sets until you have 9 blocks across.

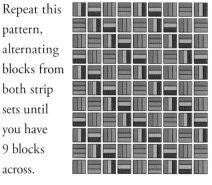

Layout and block positions

2. When beginning Row 2, you will find it easier to establish the pattern by building on a rail. The second block in Row 2 is from Strip Set B. It hooks up with the red rail established in Row 1 when its seams are vertical. The third block is another of the same block, lying horizontally. Now you know that the first block in Row 2 is from Strip Set A, lying horizontally.

3. Once you have the quilt laid out, you can again use the system of picking up all the blocks and stacking them into piles, then sewing all the rows together from those piles, as we did for *Woodland Winter,* page 35). As you are sewing, you will be able to double-check that the blocks are turned correctly, as the rails begin to form as each row grows and you will see right off when one is turned wrong.

border information for this quilt

The small inner border for this quilt is cut from the red fabric; it is ¾″ wide, finished. The outer border is cut from the green fabric; it is 4¾″ wide, finished.

Congratulations again! You have another great quilt top finished, and we trust that this is becoming easier and making more sense. You are no doubt setting up a system that works for you and keeps things in logical order. We encourage you to establish a system for yourself that keeps you efficient and accurate. This will allow you to sew faster, but precisely and accurately, without confusion and frustration.

PROJECT: CARRIE'S *PATRIOTIC LOG CABIN* QUILT

We decided to add basic Log Cabin blocks here because they are made from strips only, but not from strip sets. Many of the same principles apply, and there are endless layout patterns for Log Cabin blocks. This is just a brief introduction to sewing very square and precise blocks. If you want to explore this block further once you know how to construct the basic block accurately, you can refer to one of several books available about designing with Log Cabin blocks.

Quilt top size: 32″ × 32″ (without border)

Grid size of strip: 1″ (1½″ cut)

Block size: 8″ × 8″

Layout: 4 rows of 4 blocks each

Yardages for quilt top: See below.

DETERMINING LOG CABIN YARDAGE

To determine how many strips you will need, you will use a different process than you have up to now. Because you are not constructing strip sets that you will cut into blocks, you must determine how many strips of each color you will need to create each "log." Note: The light half of the Log Cabin block uses only one fabric, and the dark side uses three fabrics. This is an easy way to start your first Log Cabin quilt, because it keeps the math a little simpler.

Examine the block: it is built from a center square, which is surrounded by strips. The strips are nearly always divided by color, so that one diagonal half of the block is light and the other

Patriotic Log Cabin

dark. This color layout lends itself to endless design possibilities.

When constructing the block, the strips are added to the center square, working in "rounds" around the square in a circle. You will most often see blocks constructed starting with the light strips, but you can certainly start with the dark if you prefer. Below is a breakout of the pattern.

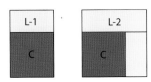

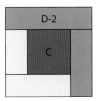

Piecing order for Log Cabin blocks

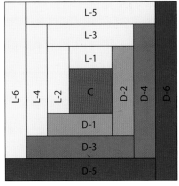

Three "rounds"

You can use the following handy chart to figure the yardage for any Log Cabin block. Just replace the center and log width measurements as needed.

Center width (cut) = 2⅝"

Log width (cut) = 1⅝"

16 blocks	Log length (before trimming)	Color	Strips needed
Log 1	2⅝"	Light	16 × 2⅝" = 42" = 1 strip
Log 2	3¾"	Light	16 × 3¾" = 60" = 2 strips
Log 3	3⅝"	Dark 1	16 × 3⅝" = 58" = 2 strips
Log 4	4⅝"	Dark 1	16 × 4⅝" = 74" = 2 strips
Log 5	4⅝"	Light	16 × 4⅝" = 74" = 2 strips
Log 6	5⅝"	Light	16 × 5⅝" = 90" = 3 strips
Log 7	5⅝"	Dark 2	16 × 5⅝" = 90" = 3 strips
Log 8	6⅝"	Dark 2	16 × 6⅝" = 106" = 3 strips
Log 9	6⅝"	Light	16 × 6⅝" = 106" = 3 strips
Log 10	7⅝"	Light	16 × 7⅝" = 122" = 3 strips
Log 11	7⅝"	Dark 3	16 × 7⅝" = 122" = 3 strips
Log 12	8⅝"	Dark 3	16 × 8⅝" = 138" = 4 strips

To figure the yardage for this quilt, you need to know that the center of the block is 2" finished, 2½" cut, and that the logs are 1" finished, 1½" cut.

To increase the accuracy of piecing, we added an extra ⅛" to each of the log strips when we cut them, so you will be able to trim them down and make them perfectly straight and square before adding each round of logs. This process is described in the instructions.

1. The center square for this quilt is 2" finished (2⅝" cut), and you need 16 of them (16 × 2⅝" = 42", or 1 strip). You need this same amount to make the first log of your quilt—that is, 1 strip of the light fabric cut 1⅝".

2. Now we are going to tally up how many strips you need of each color. For the center, we already know that you need 1 strip. For the light, you need 1 strip, 1½ strips, 2 strips, 2½ strips, 3 strips, and 3½ strips. This equals 13½ strips, or 14 strips total.

3. For the first dark you need 1½ strips and 2 strips, or 4 total. For the second dark you need 2½ and 3 strips, equaling 5½ strips, or 6 strips total, and for the third dark you need 3½ and 3½ strips, or 7 strips total.

So, here is how you figure out yardage for the quilt. For the center you need only 1 strip 2½" wide; the closest measurement a quilt shop will sell you is ⅛ yard. For the light you need 14 strips cut 1⅝" wide (14 × 1⅝" = 22¾"), which would be ⅔ or ¾ yard, depending on whether you want a little extra "just in case." For the first dark you need 4 strips; 4 × 1⅝" = 6½", or ¼ yard. For the second dark you need 6 strips; 6 × 1⅝" = 9¾", or ⅓ yard. For the third dark you need 7 strips; 7 × 1⅝" = 11⅜", or again ⅓ yard.

Final yardages for quilt top (in simpler form):

⅛ yard red fabric

⅔ or ¾ yard white fabric

¼ yard 1st dark fabric (D-1)

⅓ yard 2nd dark fabric (D-2)

⅓ yard 3rd dark fabric (D-3)

Cut:

1 strip 2⅝" wide of the red fabric

14 strips 1⅝" wide of the light fabric

4 strips 1⅝" wide of D-1

6 strips 1⅝" wide of D-2

7 strips 1⅝" wide of D-3

The basic block is constructed by joining the first light strip (L-1) to the center square (C). Rotate the center by 90° and add a second light log (L-2). Then rotate the center again and add Log 3, which will be the first dark (D-1), and rotate the center one more time to add Log 4 (D-2) to the final side. These are the first and second dark strips and the end of Round 1. Continue on, adding L-3 and L-4, then D-3 and D-4. This process keeps repeating until all the desired rounds have been added and the block is square.

CONSTRUCTING THE BLOCKS

1. Place a light strip on top of the center square fabric. Align the edges on the right side, and stitch the length of the strip. Press toward the light log.

2. With a ruler and rotary cutter, measure the size needed for the center square (2½"), and cut the length of the strips into squares. Be careful to align the ruler with the seamline, and double-check that the center square measures 2¼" from the seam to the raw edge. If it is not exact, trim it to 2¼".

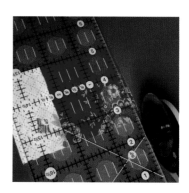

Creating centers and first log

3. Position the unit you just created on top of another light strip, making sure that the log is at the top. The seam allowance should be pressed so that its raw edges feed under the presser foot first. Stitch the first unit in place. Position another about ¼″ down the strip from the end of the first segment, and continue stitching.

Chain sewing second log

4. Continue this process until the second strip has been added to all the first units. Cut between the units to separate them, leaving a ⅛″ margin on each segment. Press closed to set the seam, then open and press toward the log.

5. At the cutting mat, with the 2 logs pointed up and to the right as you look at the block, measure with a square ruler 1¼″ from the seam allowance of both logs, and trim the extra width away. Turn the block 180° so the logs are now at the bottom and left as you look at the block. Align the 2¼″ lines on 2 sides of the ruler with the seams, and trim the center square if needed.

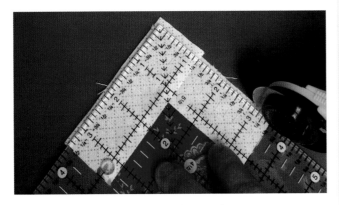
Trimming down first two logs

6. Place the 3-piece units (C, L-1, and L-2) over a strip of D-1 in the same manner as above, always making sure that the last log you sewed on—in this case, L-2—goes into the machine first (or that it is on top). Cut the units apart, and press.

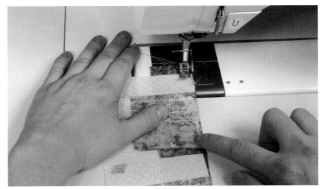
Correct log placement for sewing

7. At the cutting mat, trim the end of the log you just sewed on to be even with the center. To do this, align the 2¼″ line of the ruler with the seam directly across from the edge of the center square that has not been sewn yet. Double-check that you have a ruler line on 1 of the 2 seam allowances that run perpendicular to the left-hand seam. This will keep everything straight and square. Trim away any fabric from Log 1 (L-1), the center, or Log 3 (D-1) that extends past the ruler. You are now ready to complete the first round of the blocks.

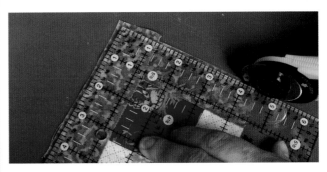
Trimming last logs for Round 1

8. Again, with the last log you added on top, place the block units on the strip for D-4, spacing them ¼″ apart. Cut apart, and press.

9. At the cutting mat, with the 2 dark logs to the top and right side, align a square ruler at 1¼″ on the logs' seamlines, and trim the top and side. Turn the block 180°. Again, measure the seams at 1¼″, and trim the top and side again.

10. You should now have the first round of logs around the center, and the block should measure 4½″. Continue stitching the units to strips, cutting them apart, pressing, squaring off the ends, trimming the logs to 1¼″ for every set of 2 like-colored logs you add, and squaring the blocks, until you have 3 complete rounds of logs.

These easy instructions are written for a quilt with logs finishing at 1″ wide. You can create a more refined-looking block by working with even smaller logs, down to ½″ wide. To figure the strip width for any other size, take your desired finished measurement, say ¾″, add ½″ for seam allowances = 1¼″, and then add an additional ⅛″ for squaring off the logs = 1⅜″.

Below is a chart of common log widths for Log Cabin blocks, the size strips you would need for the method we used above, and the size the blocks should finish to, using either a center square the same size as the logs or a center that is twice the size of the log width.

Finished log size	Cut size for log strips	Block size with a center equal in size to the logs (finished size)	Block size with a center double the size of the logs (finished size)
1½″	2⅛″	3 rounds - 10½″	3 rounds - 12″
1¼″	1⅞″	3 rounds - 8½″	3 rounds - 10″
		4 rounds - 11½″	4 rounds - 12½″
1″	1⅝″	3 rounds - 7″	3 rounds - 8″
		4 rounds - 9″	4 rounds - 10″
		5 rounds - 11″	5 rounds - 12″
¾″	1⅜″	4 rounds - 6½″	4 rounds - 7½″
		5 rounds - 8½″	5 rounds - 9″
		6 rounds - 9½″	6 rounds - 10½″
⅝″	1¼″	4 rounds - 6⅝″	4 rounds - 6½″
		5 rounds - 6⅞″	5 rounds - 7½″
		6 rounds - 8⅛″	6 rounds - 8½″
½″	1⅛″	5 rounds - 5½″	5 rounds - 6″
		6 rounds - 6½″	6 rounds - 7″

border information for this quilt

There are no borders on this quilt, but feel free to add one or two once you have read Class 180.

Class 150

Learning to draft and design your own quilts will enable you not only to make original pieces that are yours alone, but also to look at any block or quilt and be able to break it down into its basic elements, calculate the measurements to make any size quilt, and be on your way. In this chapter, we aim to get you intrigued by the elements that make a pattern happen and to get you excited about planning and mocking up your own original quilts.

Today, computer-aided drafting programs such as Electric Quilt, as well as a plethora of books and patterns, make it easy to avoid drafting. As a beginner, you can start with everything done for you except the sewing. The problem with this method of learning is that you jump into a project and do what you are told without having a true understanding of what makes it all work and fit together. If you encounter a problem, there is no answer for it in the pattern, and you are lost because you lack basic knowledge of drafting and design.

For example, Harriet is inspired by antique quilts. When she wants to make a replica, there is seldom, if ever, a pattern available. The quilt lives in a museum, out of sight, or it is pictured in a book. If she is lucky, the size of the quilt is listed in the caption. If she weren't able to assign a size to the block and build on that, she would never be able to reproduce and own a quilt that makes a room in her house shine!

Carrie is inspired by fabric. When she sees a new fabric she likes, she goes on a hunt for a pattern that feels right. However, she seldom makes the quilt exactly like the pattern. Carrie has always loved to color, and her favorite part of planning a quilt is drawing it on graph paper and coloring in the fabric colors.

To introduce you to the world of drafting and designing a quilt, we will start with the basic concepts of drafting, and in each book after this, we will add the details that are needed for the quilts addressed in that book. By the end of the series, you will be able to draft anything you want, learning the skills a bit at a time.

> **note** For now, we highly recommend that you steer clear of computer-aided design (CAD) tools. Please don't get us wrong—there are great programs available. But as a beginner, you will end up spending more time learning the ins and outs of the program than you will creating the quilt. Therefore, throughout this series of books you will be working on graph paper with colored pencils and mock-ups—a more hands-on approach.

LESSON ONE:
The basics of base grids

The key to pattern drafting lies in understanding basic patchwork structure. Most patchwork blocks are the result of dividing a square into an equal *grid* vertically and horizontally. Think of it as a checkerboard. Patchwork designs are created when squares, rectangles, and other shapes are superimposed over this base grid. Understanding base grids will help you see how a design fits together and in what order the pieces are to be sewn.

A grid is the number of squares a block pattern is divided into. Most patchwork fits into one of the four basic grid categories: four-patch, five-patch, seven-patch, and nine-patch. *The terms four-, five-, seven-, and nine-patch indicate that the block is divided into exactly that number of total divisions, or multiples of that number.* These terms have been in use for generations; you will find them repeated in every book that provides patterns according to grid category.

You will need to learn to look at a block design or pattern, and visually divide it into equal grids or units. The easiest way to do this is to create and then read the number of equal divisions across the top or down the side of the block.

If you count two, four, or eight equal divisions along the edge of the block, the block is a four-patch.

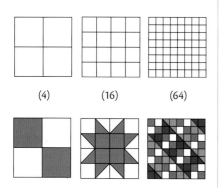

(4)   (16)   (64)

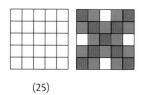

Four-patch blocks

If you count five or ten equal divisions, the block is a five-patch.

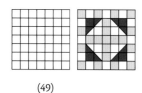

(25)

Five-patch blocks

If you count seven or fourteen equal divisions, the block is a seven-patch.

(49)

Seven-patch blocks

If you count three, six, or nine equal divisions, the block is in the nine-patch category.

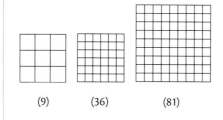

(9)   (36)   (81)

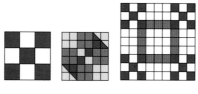

Nine-patch blocks

The lines of the base grid may not be visible in the design of the finished block. Some shapes used in a quilt block may fill more than one grid division. The Puss-in-the-Corner block is a good example.

Puss-in-the-Corner block

LESSON TWO:
Determining the grid size needed for a block

Grid size = finished size of unit

Cut size = grid size + ½″ (the seam allowances)

Always remember that drafting does not include any seam allowances.

Changing the grid size to change the block size is the basis of drafting. Let's walk through the basic steps of working with base grids.

STEP 1

Identify the base grid of the block as described. Once you understand that this grid exists, you next need to understand what to do with this information. Refer to illustrations at left.

STEP 2

Determine the block size. Let's use a simple nine-patch block for our example.

Determining block size for nine-patch block

METHOD A

Assign a measurement to the base unit and multiply it by the number of units across the block. In the illustration above, there are 3 equal divisions across the block. If each division were equal to 1″, then the finished block would be 3″ (3 divisions × 1″ = 3″). If each division were 2″, then the finished block would be 6″ (3 divisions × 2″ = 6″).

METHOD B

Pick a size that you want the finished block to be. If you select 6″ as the finished block size, divide 6″ by the number of equal divisions (in this case, 3) to determine that each individual unit is equal to 2″ (6″ ÷ 3 = 2″).

Sometimes, when you start with the block size, you pick a measurement that doesn't result in a "quilter friendly" number. For example, if you selected 8″ for the finished nine-patch, each individual unit would be equal to 2⅔″ (8″ ÷ 3 = 2⅔″). This measurement isn't easy to work with. If you don't like the answer, choose a new size and try again.

If the entire quilt is the same block, you can make the blocks almost any size you want. It's when you're making a quilt with 2 or more different block patterns that you may be confronted with the dilemma of how to work with numbers like 2⅔″. For now, let's stick with simple "happy" numbers.

STEP 3

Determine how many pattern pieces you need. To make a simple nine-patch block, you need only 1 size square. To make the Puss-in-the-Corner block, you need 2 squares of different sizes, plus a rectangle.

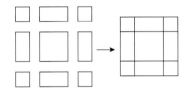

Puss-in-the Corner block

STEP 4

Determine the size of the pattern pieces. For our nine-patch block, the 6″ finished block requires a 2″ finished square. The 3″ finished block would require a 1″ finished square. (Note: We always talk in terms of finished sizes at this point.)

The Puss-in-the-Corner block is measured differently. The block is a four-patch. If we are making a 6″ fin-ished block, we need to divide the grid by 4 instead of 3 (6″ ÷ 4 = 1½″).

Each grid will finish to 1½″ instead of the 2″ in a nine-patch grid. In the first row, there are 2 squares, 1 in each corner. There are 4 corners, so you will need 4 squares 1½″ × 1½″.

The 2 center grids are actually the same fabric, which can be cut as a single unit instead of cutting 2 separate small units and sewing them together. We use the term *combined grids* for this situation (2 grids × 1½″ = 3″). If you look down the side of the block, you see that the rectangle is 1 grid wide by 2 grids long. This shape is 1½″ × 3″. There are 4 of these units in this block.

The center square is 2 grids wide and 2 grids long, making it a 3″ × 3″ square.

Now you know the finished sizes of the different block units used in these two blocks.

LESSON THREE:
Beginning drafting

Okay, you have survived the tedium of learning about grids. Here comes the fun part—you get to "go back to kindergarten" and color!

Many people think that drafting is the four-letter word of quilting. It doesn't have to be! Drafting can be as creative a process as picking the fabrics and piecing the quilt top. Here, we will begin simply and walk you though the basics of putting your layout design on paper and playing with the grid size of your quilts to see how this will affect the final product.

To begin, you are going to draft the layouts of Harriet's *Woodland Winter* or Carrie's *Cowboy Corral* from Class 130. At this point, don't worry about using graph paper with a grid that matches the grid of the quilt. Take a deep breath, and relax…we promise this will be fun!

Woodland Winter

Cowboy Corral

❊ EXERCISE: DRAWING A SIMPLE QUILT

Materials:

Graph paper (4 squares to the inch)

Basic calculator

Small see-through ruler (such as C-Thru brand, available at office or art supply stores)

Basic mechanical lead pencil

Eraser

Set of colored pencils with at least 64 colors

Drafting supplies

1. With a pencil, draw squares that are 3 graph-paper squares wide by 3 squares tall, all attached to one another. You are creating the seams of the quilt.

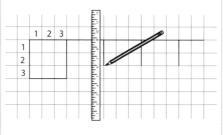

Starting to draw blocks

2. Do you see where we are getting the 3 × 3? These quilts are based on the Fence Post block and are made wholly of square blocks. The Fence Post block has 3 rails and is square, so that tells us that no matter what the finished size of the quilt, the blocks are all divisible by 3, making all the squares in the quilt 3 × 3 graph-paper grids. While we are drawing blocks, let's make our drawn quilt match the size of Harriet's quilt, so you will need 11 blocks across and 11 blocks down.

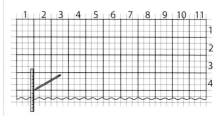

Drafting a full quilt

3. Looking at the picture of the quilt, begin to draw in the Fence Post blocks' seamlines. In this case, the pieced block is the only complicated block. You will notice in this quilt that the Fence Post blocks alternate their position. Half the time the rails run horizontally; the other half, they run vertically. While you are drawing in these seamlines, make sure you keep the pattern going the right way.

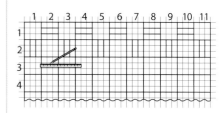

Creating the blocks

4. Now comes the fun part—you get to color! Think of it as preparation for going to the quilt shop and "petting" all those wonderful bolts of fabric! Pick your favorite colors or a color combination you like, or use 1 of the 2 color combinations from Harriet's or Carrie's quilts. Color all the Fence Post blocks, first mimicking the color layout of 1 of the 2 quilts.

5. Next, color the solid alternate blocks. In Harriet's quilt, there are 2 different colors of alternate blocks that create a secondary pattern. In Carrie's quilt, they are all the same color. Compare the drawings below to see how the different placement of color in the blocks can change the feeling and look of the quilt.

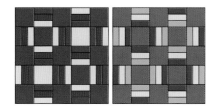

Woodland Winter   Cowboy Corral

Color layouts for Harriet's quilt (left)
and Carrie's quilt (right)

6. Try doing a few drawings placing different colors of the solid alternate square in different configurations. What happens when you color the Fence Post block differently? Do you like the quilt better?

Remember that when you choose fabric, you are not committed to the color you have used on your drawing. Say you have chosen three colors of blue for your rail blocks and two purples for your solid square blocks. Perhaps you decide that the Fence Post blocks look too "blah" with only three shades of the same color. Instead of redrawing and recoloring the whole

quilt, wait until you get to the quilt shop and find a fabric that "speaks" to you. Imagine where that fabric will fit with your drawing. Note in the drawing which color you are substituting this fabric for, and build from there.

Let the fabric you fall in love with determine what your quilt will ultimately look like.

❋ EXERCISE: DRAWING A MORE COMPLEX QUILT

Now that you have drawn an easy quilt, let's draw out another, slightly more challenging quilt. Carrie's *Interlacing Circles* is a quilt you will be making in Class 160 page 75).

1. Look closely at this quilt. You will notice that it is the same 3 × 3 grid as Rail Fence. To begin, draw 7 grid blocks, 3 × 3, across the paper and 7 grid blocks down, using 3 squares of the graph paper for each.

2. Next, draw the most complicated block: the Nine-Patch. There should be a total of 16 Nine-Patch blocks in

your drawing—every other block in every other row.

3. Draw in the seamlines for the rail blocks.

4. Now you're ready to color. This quilt's color placement can be confusing. To achieve the interlacing circle effect, you have 2 different sets of rails…see them in the photo? If not, refer to the drawing below to see how this color placement creates the design.

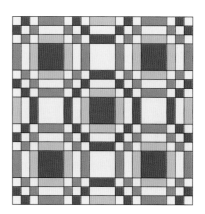

Interlacing Circles drawings with color placement exaggerated

Carrie's *Interlacing Circles*

✻ EXERCISE: DRAWING A COMBINED GRID QUILT

The third quilt we will walk through together to draw is Harriet's *Irish Chain Variation* quilt from Class 170, Lesson Four page 90). It's an example of a *combined grid* quilt, meaning that sections of each block have areas that are two, three, or four times the width or length (or both) of the grid of the quilt. Because the blocks in combined grid quilts are not as easy to discern as those in simpler quilts, it is important that you learn early on to break apart these less obvious block designs.

1. Count how many grid units there are across the quilt (start counting at the widest part of the colorful blocks). Did you get 25? If not, did you count the white areas as 1 or 2 grids?

2. Look at how many "blocks" there are across the quilt. Did you count 5 (3 "scrappy" blocks and 2 blue-and-white blocks)? If so, you have 25 grids divided between 5 blocks, making each block 5 grids wide. Since the blocks are square, you know they are a five-patch grid.

3. Let's draw the first row. Draw 5 blocks with 5 squares in each across the graph paper.

4. Draw in the seamlines. In the "scrappy" blocks (Block A), the first row of the block has a white rectangle, a colored square, and another white rectangle. Draw that in. Don't divide the large solid areas with seams, no matter the division of the block, until you have the whole block diagrammed. When you go back and start thinking about how to piece the block(s), you can make the decision as

Irish Chain Variation

to whether and where those areas need seams.

Block A: *Irish Chain Variation*

5. In the blue-and-white blocks (Block B) the first row has a blue square, a white rectangle, and then another blue square. Note that both the left and right sides of the block also have large white rectangles running down the sides. Again, don't draw in the seamlines in those rectangles.

6. Continue drawing out Row 1, and finish by drawing out the whole quilt…easy enough, right?

Block B: *Irish Chain Variation*

The elements in this quilt are what make it a combined grid, in which sections of each block have areas that are two, three, or four times the width or length (or both) of the grid of the quilt. "Combining" the grids of these areas into one results in less sewing and a more pleasing look to the finished piece. You will learn more about combined grids in Class 170 (page 86).

❋ EXERCISE: CHANGING GRID SIZES

Continue to practice by drafting out the various quilts in this book to get an idea of how to correctly identify the blocks in the quilts and the color placement. Once you get the hang of it, you can start to play with the block orientation. Following are two examples of Carrie's *Country Lanes* table runner (page 60). You can see that simply changing the placement of the four-patches changes the secondary pattern in the table runner.

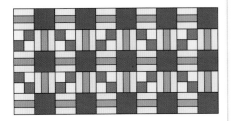

Country Lanes blocks laid out as table runner

Country Lanes blocks laid out square for quilt

By now, you have the basic idea of how to get a picture of a quilt you like transferred onto graph paper. By looking at the elements of the quilt, you can assign a grid size to them to get the size quilt you want to make. The nice thing about working on 4- or 8-to-the-inch graph paper is that you can simply assign each of those squares a grid size, regardless of the grid of the graph paper.

Go back to the drawing you did of either Harriet's or Carrie's quilt in Exercise: Drawing a simple quilt (page 51), and let's play around with grid sizes. We are going to start big, so let's assign each square of the graph paper a size of 2″. This should be easy for you to work out.

If each graph paper square equals 2″, and each block is 3 squares by 3 squares, then 2″ × 3 = 6″ (this is the finished size of the blocks for your quilt). Now look on a ruler. Does 2″ seem a little chunky to you? Well, let's try 1½″. Do the same math: 1½″ × 3 = 4½″. Does that seem a little nicer? How about a little smaller yet—let's try 1¼″. That's 1¼″ × 3 = 3¾″. Play with the math to your heart's content.

For *Cowboy Corral*, Carrie did not pick the size of her blocks first. The pictures in the fabric she chose for the solid squares dictated the size those blocks needed to be, and then she sized the Fence Post blocks to fit. In that fabric, the motif squares measured 3½″ × 3½″. She calculated 3½″ ÷ 3 = 1.16″, but that was not a quilter-friendly number. By using a square ruler, you can size up the square to be divisible by three. With *Cowboy Corral*, the solid blocks were cut 5″ so that the finished size would be 4½″. This is a special case. If you look at *Interlacing Circles*, you will notice that again there are large solid squares, but this time you are able to determine the size you want your Nine-Patch and Fence Post blocks to be and then simply cut the fabric you are using for the solid squares to the size you need.

All right! You have the basics of drafting! Not too hard, was it? In Class 170, you will start the process of figuring yardage, so keep your drawings and set them aside to use as worksheets when you get there.

LESSON FOUR:
Making fabric mock-ups of blocks

Now it's time to go one step further in the quilt planning process. Once you have chosen the fabrics you think you want to work with, you might want to buy ⅛ yard of each to experiment with before buying large quantities. There are different ways to experiment. Some quilters are okay with just cutting fabric and charging right into a project, making the whole quilt a bit of an experiment, while others like the security of seeing the quilt first by making mock-up blocks.

If you buy ⅛-yard pieces of fabric, remember that fabric can sell out fast, so make your mock-up as soon as possible. If you are purchasing the fabric anyway, buy an extra ⅛ yard to play with. If you are working out of your stash of fabric and are afraid you may run short, you can make a color photocopy of the fabric and use that, without actually cutting into the fabric. Either way, it is a small investment to make in order to be sure that your quilt turns out just the way you envisioned it!

✳ EXERCISE: MAKING A MOCK-UP

Materials:

Large pad of 18″ × 24″ graph paper (4-to-the-inch)

⅛ yard of each fabric in the block(s)

To make a mock-up block or blocks of a quilt to scale, work with 4-to-the-inch graph paper. This is where a large pad of graph paper will come in extremely handy. We will be using Carrie's *Country Lanes* table runner (below) for this first project.

1. Determine the grid of the quilt, which is 1″. Because the Fence Post blocks are the smallest scale, start by drawing these blocks. On the graph paper, draw at least 2, if not 3, squares 3″ × 3″.

Drawing block to scale

2. Draw in the seams, just as we did in the previous exercise, starting with the most "complicated" block.

Country Lanes table runner

3. Cut strips or photocopies of fabric the size of the squares or rectangles that are now marked on the graph paper, and glue them in place according to the color layout you think you want to work with.

Gluing fabric to mock-up block

Gluing photocopied fabric to mock-up block

> *tip* If you just don't have much fabric or access to a color photocopier, make the blocks to scale but in a reduced grid. For example, if your quilt is a 1″ grid, mock it up in a ½″ or even a ¼″ grid, as Harriet did when she was working on her *Town Square* quilt for this book.

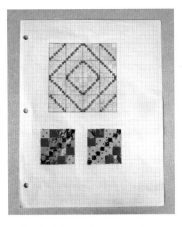

Harriet's *Town Square* mock-up

Whichever method you use, take some time with these first quilts, and do the drafting and block mock-ups. It's a fun and easy way to build your confidence in drafting and color selection for all your quilts.

Planning a quilt layout

Many quilts will never see a bed. They hang on the wall, cover the dining room table, or keep the baby warm in the car seat. Many others are made just because we wanted to work in certain colors, and we weren't too concerned about the size of the finished product. But what happens when you want to make a quilt for a particular bed or need the quilt to finish a particular size? How do you plan it?

About now, we realize that you may be thinking that it would be easier just to buy a pattern or book and be done with it! All the work and decisions have already been made! However, when you rely on patterns, you're not developing the skills that will enable you to take a picture or conceive an idea and work it through to make it a reality.

Our goal is to teach you to look at a quilt and assign a desired size to it, figure out what size block is needed to accommodate that size, and go forward. We want you to be confident enough in design that you don't feel the only way to make a quilt larger is to add more borders, regardless of their proportions and suitability.

In order to have a structure to work with, you first need to determine what size the finished quilt will be.

* Is the quilt for a bed? What size is the bed?

* How far do you want the quilt to hang over the edges—to the mattress, a few inches over the dust ruffle, or to the floor?

* Do you need a pillow tuck, or will shams be on top of the quilt?

* Is the quilt for a wall? If so, what dimensions are needed to fill the space adequately?

DETERMINING THE NUMBER OF BLOCKS

Once you know what size the quilt needs to be, choose any pattern in the book and find the block or blocks that make up the layout. The quilts in this book are all simple *straight set* layouts, meaning that the blocks sit side by side and are parallel to the outside edges of the quilt. This makes the quilt easy to size.

Divide the width of the quilt by the width of the quilt block to determine the number of blocks in a horizontal row. Now divide the quilt length by the length of the quilt block to determine the number of blocks in a vertical row.

You will find that these rarely come out even. This is when you need to decide whether to (a) enlarge the overall quilt size in order to use the quilt block in the chosen size, (b) add borders so that the chosen quilt block can be used, or (c) resize the quilt block itself.

Let's walk through an example. The *Triple Rail Fence* quilt in Class 140 is a simple straight set. The quilt is small, with a fairly small grid. What if you wanted to make this into a sofa throw about 58″ square? If the blocks are 3¾″ × 3¾″ as in the project, you would divide 58″ by 3.75″ to get 15.46. That would be 15 or 16 blocks across and 15 or 16 rows, needing at least 225 blocks to fill the space. That's a lot of blocks, and the grid size might look too small and busy for a larger quilt.

Let's change the block size. If you use a 2″ grid, the blocks would be 6″ square. For a 58″ square throw, figure 58″ ÷ 6″ = 9.67. That would be 9 or 10 blocks in each of 9 or 10 rows. Let's go with 9 blocks. That would require 81 blocks. However, you might find that the 6″ blocks look bulky, and you want something a bit smaller.

The first example was a 1¼″ grid and the second a 2″ grid. Let's split the difference and try a 1½″ grid. That would make the blocks 4½″ square. Figure 58″ ÷ 4.5″ = 12.88, or 13 blocks in each of 13 rows. That requires 169 blocks.

This is all fairly simple when you understand grids and how every block can be changed to meet the needs of the quilt you are planning.

Any of the quilts in this book can easily be made larger or smaller by simply changing the size of the grid to accommodate the new size you want. A perfect example is the 48″ × 64″ *Asian Nights* quilt (page 66). It was created by simply adding more blocks to the 32″ × 32″ *Town Square* quilt (page 63). If you didn't want to make more blocks with the 1″ grid used in the project, the grid size could be increased by ¼″ or ½″ to make the blocks larger. This would require less sewing, and the larger blocks would fill more space more quickly.

Design is very personal, and once you start to explore how grid size and setting affect the look of the final project, you will be able to fill any needs you have with each of your projects. If you want to make a quilt quickly, increase the

grid, and therefore the block size. If you love detail, use a smaller block, and add more of them for a larger size. The choice will be all yours.

---

terminology to know

Grid: the finished size of the unit

Cut size: the grid size plus ½″ for seam allowances

Block A: the block with the most seams or smallest pieces in the quilt

Block B: a block with fewer seams and pieces than the A block, or a different color layout

---

LESSON SIX:
Expanding piecing skills with Four-Patch blocks

As you progress through the rest of the quilts in this book, we will look at what units make the blocks, how to break the blocks apart to start construction, and how to determine how many strips to cut and sew for each unit. We are not going to just present a recipe for cutting and sewing. We want you to start thinking through the entire process so that you know where we got our measurements and numbers. Once you work through this next set of quilts, you will be better prepared to understand the yardage calculations taught in Class 170. You'll also have a better understanding of all the drafting "mumbo jumbo" we talked about at the beginning of this class.

❋ EXERCISE: CONSTRUCTING FOUR-PATCH BLOCKS FOR THE SAMPLER QUILT

This exercise will refresh the skills you learned in the Fence Post exercise (page 27)—cutting, sewing, pressing, and butting seams, as well as chain piecing. The four-patch units we make here will be the corner blocks for the sampler quilt. The exercise will also prepare you for making the next quilt projects.

MAKING THE STRIP SETS

1. Cut 2 strips 2″ wide from both the light and the dark fabric. Stitch a dark and a light strip together, making sure the edges align exactly. Repeat to create a second strip set.

2. Do you remember the pressing sequence (page 26)? Using steam, first press the strips closed as they came off the machine to set the seams, then press the seams to one side. Finally, lightly spray the pieces with starch—up to 3 times—so they are flat and sharply creased.

3. Check the width of the strips by measuring off the seam, as we have done in each previous project. Refer to page 28 for a reminder. The strips should be exactly 1¾" wide from the seam. If there is a narrow space, that will need to be cut out. If there are any wide spaces, trim the edge to achieve the exact 1¾".

4. Now cut the strip sets into segments. Using a ruler, place a cross line on the seam (you have turned the strip to lie left to right on the mat), and square off one end. The cut end and the seam should be exactly perpendicular to each other at a true 90° angle.

Strip cut into segments

5. Rotate the strip set and start cutting from this trimmed end. Align the 2" line on the ruler with the cut edge, and be sure that the cross line on the ruler is exactly on top of the seam. Cut. Repeat this until you have 32 segments 2" wide.

6. Divide the 32 segments into 2 stacks of 16, with 1 stack turned the opposite direction from the other so that you have a checkerboard effect.

Rotate to form checkerboard.

tip When laying out the units, have the raw edges of the seam allowances of the right-hand stack leading into the machine. As the units go through the machine, the pressure of the foot will push the top seam allowance into the bottom one, giving you a better chance to perfectly butt the seam. The pieces don't always let you do this, but when they do, it can really help accuracy.

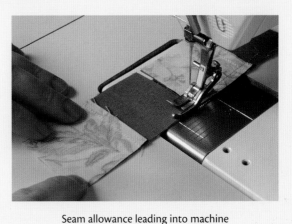

Seam allowance leading into machine

SEWING THE BLOCKS

1. Lay the stacks to the right side of your machine. Pick up 1 segment from the left stack with your left hand and 1 from the right stack with your right hand, and pair them together—right (2) on top of left (1)…remember? Be sure that the seam locks (butts or nests) together over the entire length of the seam. Hold the seams together and stitch the segments together. Pick up 2 more units, place 2 on top of 1, butting or nesting seams, and stitch. There should be a ¼" chain of thread between the 2 units now. Continue with this system until you have 16 pairs stitched together.

2. Open the units and check for perfectly butted seams. If any are not butted dead-on, take out the stitches and repeat until you are successful. Pin if necessary, as discussed in Class 130, page 31.

FANNING THE **SEAMS**

If the seams are pressed to one side, a lump will be created by the seams lying on top of one another. There is a really slick way to eliminate this by "fanning" the seams.

❋ With the four-patch wrong side up, position it so that the seam you just stitched is parallel to you (running left to right). You will notice that the top left square has no seam allowance pressed onto it; neither does the lower right square. We are going to push the horizontal seam toward these 2 squares, splitting the stitches in the center.

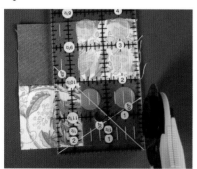

Seam parallel to your body

❋ Place your thumbs on either side of the center vertical seam, pushing the seam allowance up on the left side and down on the right side.

Twist to open stitches.

❋ Twist your thumbs slightly while you do this, and the stitches in the seam will release, allowing the seam allowances to lie in 2 different directions. You should get a tiny four-patch in the very center where all the seams meet.

Correctly fanned seam

❋ To press, turn the block over to the right side and press one side in the direction the seam allowance is lying, then rotate the block and press the other seam. Do this gently, using the point of the iron. Lightly starch. The block will be flat with no lump in the center.

Any time you have checkerboard-like four-patch and nine-patch blocks, you can use this technique. Would you always use it? Not necessarily, nor can you always use it. But once you know how to do it, you can determine for yourself when the reduction of bulk is a big plus.

---

3. Again check the width of each side of the blocks. Measure from the seam to the raw edge of the units, and trim if necessary. Square from both seams so you know that the block is perfectly square as you trim. You can either use a straight ruler and do 1 side at a time, or use a square ruler and check 2 sides at once. Check all 4 sides of each block. The blocks should now be exactly 3½" square, 1¾" from each seam.

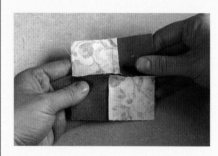

Ruler line placement to check size

4. The corner blocks of the sampler are made up of 4 four-patch units joined together. Using the photo on page 27 as a guide, lay out 1 corner (4 units) and stack up the other 3 corners on top of these. You will now construct all the corner blocks at once.

5. Pick up the left top unit and place the right top unit on top of it. Align and butt all the seams to ensure that the block stays square. Stitch the right edge. Repeat with the next units in these stacks 3 more times, until the stacks are gone. You have now joined the top units of all 4 blocks. Repeat this process for the remaining 2 stacks.

Stacking four corner blocks at once

6. At the ironing board, fan the seam intersections and press the seams of all 8 half-blocks. Starch lightly.

7. At the machine, lay out the 2 rows, each 4 units deep, and stitch the rows together. The seam intersections of this long seam will also be fanned. Press and starch this seam. You now have 4 corner blocks, each containing 16 squares, 1½″ × 1½″, creating a checkerboard.

8. Again, measure off the outside seams, and make sure that the small squares along the outside edges of the blocks are exactly 1¾″, and that each block is exactly 6½″ square. If you have achieved this, you will have no problem constructing the following quilts. If you have encountered problems with this exercise, repeat it until you find where the problems are.

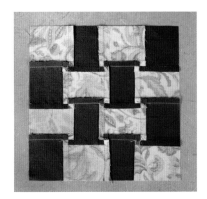

All seams fanned

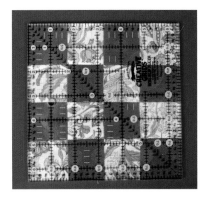

Sides are 1¾″; block is exactly 6½″ square.

Our goal is to have you learn to slow down, take a breath, and enjoy the process of piecing. This is not a race. You will save hours of time ripping and much frustration if you will take the time to learn accuracy from the very start. Once you learn to quilt, you will be amazed at how easy it is to quilt a well-pieced, well-pressed top with seams that make the back of the quilt top as neat as the front.

PIECING **CHECKLIST**

Make sure the strips are cut accurately from the yardage. If the strips aren't cut accurately, nothing else will fall into place. Review Class 120, Lesson Five, page 19.

✻ Straight stitching is critical. If you are having problems sewing a straight seam, do you have a barrier-type seam guide on your machine? Are you looking at the guide and not the foot when sewing? Straight stitching is mandatory for accurate piecing. Experiment with different feet and seam guides before going any further, and practice until you are able to sew a straight seam. Review the information about presser feet in Class 130, Lessons One to Three, pages 20–25.

✻ Check your pressing. All too often, the cutting and sewing are accurate, but the pressing is poor. If the strips are wavy and look stretched, you are likely pulling on the strips as you are pressing them. This causes the fabric to stretch. Let the iron do the work. You are not pressing with an up-and-down motion; you are actually pushing against the sewn seam with the edge of the iron. Be sure not to use the point of the iron, as it will stretch the fabric. Steam will soften the fabric so that it will move easily, but be careful not to steam too much. The fabric should not be damp.

✻ If the units or blocks are not square, did you remember to measure and trim the strips after each step of the construction? It is common to skip this step, as it seems tedious and redundant, but if the units are not square and straight, and you sew two of them together, the problems start to snowball and the end result is blocks that are not square and straight.

Four-Patch quilts
PROJECT: CARRIE'S *COUNTRY LANES* TABLE RUNNER

Country Lanes

Quilt top size: 15″ × 66″ (without borders)

Grid size of smallest unit: 1″

Block size: 3″ × 3″

Blocks:

49 Rail Fence blocks

18 Four-Patch blocks

36 solid blocks

Layout: 5 rows of 19 blocks each (95 total), plus the 2 graduated ends of 4 blocks each (8 total), for a grand total of 103 blocks

Yardages for quilt top:

½ yard cream floral print fabric

¼ yard light green print fabric

⅛ yard tan tonal fabric

⅛ yard brown print fabric

⅓ yard large-scale green floral fabric

½ yard large-scale green floral fabric for border

Three different blocks make up the design: a Rail Fence block, which you perfected in Class 140; a Four-Patch block, which you just mastered; and a solid block.

Rail Fence block

Four-Patch block

Solid block

Three blocks used in *Country Lanes*

MAKING THE RAIL FENCE BLOCKS

Which block do you cut your fabric for first? Normally, you would start with the easiest block and then move on to the hardest. But in this case, we will start with the Rail Fence block—the one with the smallest grid. These blocks are constructed like the Fence Post blocks you made for the sampler quilt (page 27) and have only two fabrics instead of three fabrics, as in the quilts in Classes 130 and 140. So, how many strips do you need to cut to make the Rail Fence blocks? There are two strips of the cream floral in each block and only one strip of the light green print.

Cut:

9 strips 1½″ wide of the cream floral print fabric

5 strips 1½″ wide of the light green print fabric

Wonder how we arrived at these numbers? Well, you need 49 Rail Fence blocks for this quilt. The cream fabric appears twice in the block and the green fabric only once, so right there you know that you will need half as many strips of the green as you will the cream.

Let's figure for the cream. There are 49 blocks, each of which has 2 cream units, so 49 × 2 = 98 units of cream needed. One strip yields 12 units. Each block is cut 3½" square, so 98 units ÷ 12 = 8.16 strips needed, rounded up to 9 strips.

For the green fabric, figure on 49 blocks, and 1 green unit per 3½"-square block. The math would be: 49 ÷ 12 = 4.08 strips needed. Round this up to 5, but you will actually need 4 strips plus a bit more of green. Cut a cream strip in half so you have 8 full strips and 2 half strips, which will give you a total of 4½ strip sets for the Rail Fence blocks.

1. Sewing the strips together for this quilt is no different than sewing the strips for *Woodland Winter* (page 33). There are just fewer of them, and only 2 colors. Lay out the strips beside your machine in the following order: cream-green-cream.

2. Place a green strip on top of a cream strip and sew them together. Continue until all of the first stack of cream strips and all of the green strips are gone. Sew the half strip last. Press the seams toward the green, starch, measure, and correct as necessary. Each strip should measure 1¼".

3. Sew the other cream strip to the green side of the strip set. Press again toward the green strip, starch, and measure for accuracy. The finished

strip set should measure 3½" wide down the entire length of each strip set.

4. To cut the blocks, align a ruler with both of the internal seams of a strip set, and cut off the selvage end of the strip, creating a straight line to measure from. Turn the strip around and measure 3½" from this edge, using the seams and ruler lines to keep everything aligned perfectly.

5. Cut 49 Rail Fence blocks 3½" × 3½". Set these aside.

MAKING THE FOUR-PATCH BLOCKS

Cut:

> 2 strips 2" wide of the tan tonal fabric
>
> 2 strips 2" wide of the brown print fabric

To figure out how we got these numbers, follow along again. There are 18 Four-Patch blocks in this quilt, and each is made up of 2 strips—a tan fabric and a brown print fabric. There are 2 segments of the tan and brown in each block; 18 blocks × 2 segments = 36, so you will need to cut 36 segments from the strip sets. Each segment will be cut 2" wide. Remember that the grid size is 1", as established by the Rail Fence block, which is divided into 3, making the finished block size 3". Four-Patch blocks are only divided by 2, so 3" blocks ÷ 2 units = 1½" grid plus ½" for seam allowance = 2".

You need 36 segments, each cut 2" wide. Each 42" strip yields 21 units 2" wide. 36 ÷ 21 units = 1.71, or 2 strips. That is how you figure out that you need 2 strips each of the tan and the brown print.

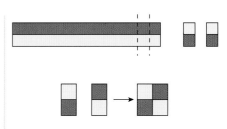

Four-Patch strip set

1. Sew both strips of brown to both strips of tan. Press the seam allowances toward the brown strips. Starch lightly. Check for strip width accuracy. The strips should be 1¾" from the seam to the raw edge. The total strip width should measure 3½". If it does not, check your seam allowance and pressing for any problems, and correct if necessary.

2. Cut the segments for the four-patches. Using the techniques you learned in the exercise in Lesson Six (page 56), cut 36 segments 2" wide from the strip sets.

3. Make 2 stacks of 18 segments each, and turn 1 stack to be opposite the other to form a four-patch. Lay out the colors so that the brown square is at the top of the segments in the right stack.

4. Place 1 segment from the right-hand stack on top of 1 segment from the left-hand stack. Remember the #2 on top of #1 rule? Refer to Making the strip sets in the *Triple Rail Fence* project (page 42) as a reminder.

5. Place the segments under the machine and start to stitch. They are aligned properly if the brown is on top and leading in, and the raw edge of the seam allowance is heading toward the presser foot. Do not deviate from this. *The brown square must be on top and under the machine first every time.* Refer to the photo on page 57 as a reminder.

6. Continue chain sewing the units together until you have 18 pairs sewn together. Check that every seam is perfectly butted, and press, fanning the intersecting seams as you did on the sampler Four-Patch blocks (page 58).

7. Square up each four-patch unit. Lay the 1¾" line of the ruler on the seam and trim all 4 sides, 1 at a time, to ensure that every four-patch is exactly 3½" square.

8. You now have 18 Four-Patch blocks. Set these aside.

Making the solid blocks

Cut:

4 strips 3½" wide of the large-scale green floral fabric

Here is the last bit of math for this quilt, and it is easy! You need 36 solid blocks, and these blocks need to be cut 3½" square. Each 42" strip yields 12 units. So, 36 ÷ 12 = 3 strips of fabric needed. Cut these strips into 3½" segments until you have 36 solid squares. You are now ready to lay out your table runner and sew it together.

1. Lay out the blocks as shown in the layout diagram.

2. Now you can again use the system of picking up all the blocks and making stacks as described in Constructing Fence Posts, page 29. You will find it easier to sew the table runner together if you have only 5 rows down and 19 rows across, and then sew all the rows together from those stacks, as we did in all the previous projects (except for the Log Cabin). You can then construct the 4 end pieces separately. As you are sewing, you will be able to double-check that the blocks are turned correctly, because the Rail Fence and Four-Patch blocks will begin to form a pattern as each row grows. You will notice right off if one is turned wrong.

3. If you want to create the diagonal ends for this table runner, you will now need to sew together the blocks for the 2 ends.

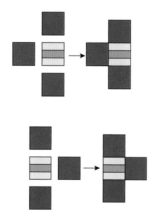

End pieces for table runner

4. Sew these end pieces to the constructed table runner. To create the diagonal cut, turn the quilt to the right side and align the ¼" line of a ruler with the seam junction of the Rail Fence and solid blocks that make up the end of the table runner. This will give you a ¼" seam allowance to sew the border onto when you are ready.

Ruler placement for trimming down table runner

border information for this quilt

There is a single border on this table runner that has been mitered in 6 places to create the triangles at both ends. The border finishes to be 3" wide.

You've done it! You've made a great table runner to dress up any table, and it was easy to make, right? Now on to the next, more challenging quilt!

note *Borders will be discussed and yardage determined in Class 180. Please do not skip ahead. Just fold all of the quilt tops you have made so far and lay them aside until toward the end of this course.*

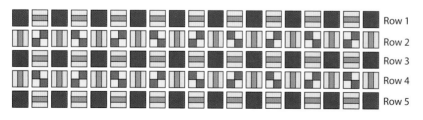

Row 1
Row 2
Row 3
Row 4
Row 5

Block layout for *Country Lanes*

PROJECT: HARRIET'S *TOWN SQUARE* QUILT

Quilt top size: 32″ × 32″ (without borders)

Grid size of smallest unit: 1″

Block size: 8″ × 8″

Blocks:

8 Block A

8 Block B

Layout: 4 rows of 4 blocks each

Yardages for quilt top:

½ yard tan fabric

⅓ yard pink fabric

½ yard green print fabric

⅜ yard dark green fabric

¼ yard dark green fabric for inner border

⅝ yard green print fabric for outer border

In this quilt, each block contains 2 large and 2 small four-patch units. The blocks are referred to as Block A and Block B; they are different only in their fabric color placement. You can make both blocks at the same time if you are careful to keep the color placement correct. It is always a good idea to make a mock-up of these blocks, either with colored pencils or tiny snippets of fabric, so that you can easily refer to a sample that shows fabric and color placement (see Making a mock-up, page 55).

Town Square

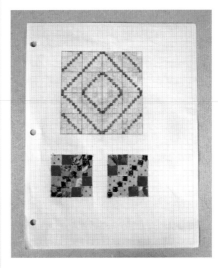

Mock-up of color placement

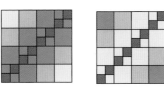

Block A   Block B

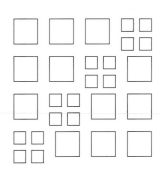

Block broken out into units

> *note* It is extremely important to remember this from here on out: always start by making the smallest unit in the quilt first.

MAKING THE FOUR-PATCH UNITS

For this quilt, the smallest units are the small four-patch units in both blocks. When it is separated out from the block, you will see that this four-patch is made from 2 strips, each cut 1½″ wide. We have an established 1″ grid, plus ½″ for seam allowance.

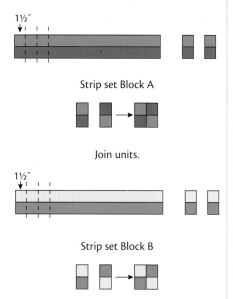

Strip set Block A

Join units.

Strip set Block B

First strips and segments to make

How many strips do we need for the small four-patch units? Let's start with Block A. There are 8 of Block A, and 4 small four-patch units in each block. It takes 2 segments—each 1½″ long—to make each small four-patch. Let's do a bit of math to see exactly how many strips we need to sew to accommodate the small four-patch units needed.

Four four-patch units per block = 2 segments for each unit = 8 segments. Each segment is a 1½″ cut. There are 8 blocks and 8 segments each = 64 units total. Each 42″ strip yields 28 units 1½″ wide. 64 ÷ 28 = 2.28 strips needed, rounded up to 3 strips.

Block B strips and yardage are figured in exactly the same way.

Cut:

6 strips 1½″ wide of dark green fabric (4 for Block A, 4 for Block B)

3 strips 1½″ wide of green print fabric for Block A

3 strips 1½″ wide of tan fabric for Block B

1. Sew together 4 strips of dark green fabric and 4 strips of light green fabric. Press the seam allowances toward the dark green strips. Starch lightly. Check for strip width accuracy. The strips should be 1¼″ from the seam to the raw edge. The total strip width should measure 2½″. Correct any problems. If you are making both blocks at the same time, sew 4 strips of dark green to 4 strips of tan in the same way.

2. Using the ruler lines to align perfectly with the seam, trim off the right end of a strip set, removing the selvage and squaring the strip set. Cut segments as in Step 2 for Making the Four-Patch blocks, page 57. Cut 64 segments 1½″ wide from each color combination.

3. Make 2 stacks of 32 segments each, and turn 1 stack to be opposite the other to form a four-patch. Lay out the colors so that the dark green square is at the top of the segment on the right stack.

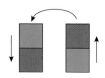

Dark green on top right, #2 on top of #1

4. Place 1 segment from the right-hand pile on top of 1 segment from the left-hand pile as in Making the Four-Patch blocks, page 57. Place the segments under the presser foot, and

start to stitch. They are aligned properly if the dark green is on top and leading in, and the raw edge of the seam allowance is heading toward the presser foot. Do not deviate from this. *The dark green square must be on top and under the machine first every time.*

Chain stitching with same color square always leading into machine

5. Repeat for the Block B color combination. Check that every seam is perfectly butted, and fan the intersecting seams as you press, as you did for the sampler Four-Patch blocks, page 58.

6. Square up all the four-patch units. Lay the 1¼″ line of the ruler on the seam, and trim all 4 sides, 1 at a time, to ensure that every four-patch is exactly 2½″ square. You now have 32 small four-patch units each for Blocks A and B.

MAKING THE A AND B BLOCKS

Refer back to the block illustrations (page 63), and you will see that the four-patches are attached to a square of the same fabric that is opposite the dark green in each four-patch combination. Instead of cutting and sewing squares onto squares, we can attach the four-patches to a strip. This will allow you to square off from the seam and keep the 2 pieces in perfect alignment.

You need 32 squares from strips of 2 colors for both Block A and B—each 2½″ wide. So, 42″ (strip length) ÷ 2.5″ (unit length) = 16.8, and 32 (units needed) ÷ 16 (units per strip) = 2 strips.

Cut:

2 strips 2½″ wide of the green print fabric

2 strips 2½″ wide of the tan fabric

1. Starting with the light green strip lying face up, position a Block A four-patch on top, right sides together. *Always have the dark green square of the four-patch at the top right corner.* Stitch the right side onto the strip. Leave about ¼″ of strip, and position another four-patch unit, making sure that the dark green square is in the top right position.

2. Continue with all 32 four-patches and both strips. If you run short of the wide strips, cut enough to finish. This might happen because of too much space between the four-patch units.

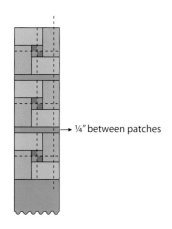

→ ¼″ between patches

Four-patches being sewn onto a strip

3. Using scissors, cut between the ¼″ space that separates the units. Press the seam toward this large piece and starch lightly. Using a ruler, align with the seams and the cut edge of the four-patch, and cut the wide strip unit to exactly 2½″ wide. You will have 32 units 4½″ × 2½″.

4. Repeat Steps 1 through 3 for Block B, using 2 strips 2½″ wide of tan fabric.

5. Using the units you have made, make 2 stacks of 16 units, 1 turned opposite the other. Stitch these together; then fan the intersecting seam, and press the seams flat.

Units stitched and trimmed

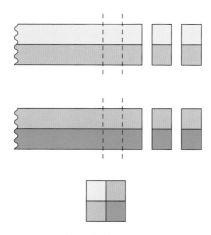

Pressing is neat and tidy on back.

6. Repeat for Block B. You now have half of the quilt top finished.

7. For the second half of the block, only 2½″ strips are needed. The pink is used in each strip set.

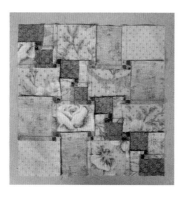

Color order for strip sets

8. You will need to make 32 of these units. There are 2 in each block, and

16 blocks total. They are the same for each block, just positioned differently. For each color combination and strip set, you will need 32 units, each 2½″ long. So, 42″ ÷ 2.5″ = 16.8, and 42″ strip length ÷ 16 = 2 strips. You will need to make 2 strip sets of each combination.

Cut:

2 strips 2½″ wide of the tan fabric

2 strips 2½″ wide of the green print fabric

4 strips 2½″ wide of the pink fabric

9. Sew 2 tan and 2 pink strips together. Press toward the tan.

10. Sew 2 green print and 2 pink strips together. Press toward the green print. Check that each strip is exactly 2¼″ wide from the seam.

11. Cut each color-combination strip set into 32 segments 2½″ long. Lay out the segments in 2 stacks of 32, with the pink corners opposite each other. Stitch them together, fan the seams, and press. Square up with a ruler to make every side of each square exactly 2½″. You are now ready to lay out the units to make the blocks.

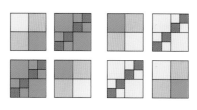

Block A layout   Block B layout

12. Stitch the first block of Row 1 to the second block. When aligning, make sure all seams, both vertical and horizontal throughout the units, butt properly. By aligning all the seams, you are ensuring that the block stays square. Continue until all 8 Block A units in Row 1 have been joined.

13. Repeat with Row 2. Fan seam allowances. Stitch Row 1 to Row 2, matching and butting every seam.

14. Repeat this process for Block B. Check against Block A for direction to press seams. You will plan the direction the seams will be pressed for Block B once the blocks are laid out in the pattern of the quilt.

ASSEMBLING THE QUILT TOP

Once all the A and B blocks are constructed, lay out the

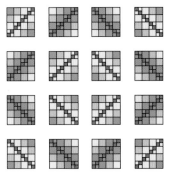

Quilt layout

blocks on a table, the floor, or a bed, and work out the pattern of the chains. If you don't like the original color placement, it can be reversed at this point. Play with placement until you are totally satisfied. Examine all the seams to be sure the blocks are positioned so that all interior seams lie in opposite directions and are ready to butt together. By planning this way, you can determine which direction the final seam should be pressed.

To stitch the blocks together, we are going to work in another four-patch configuration. Divide the quilt top into quarters. There will be 4 blocks in each corner. You will be stitching the first 2 blocks, then the second 2 blocks, and then joining them together into a big four-patch. By doing this instead of sewing long rows together, you have more control over seam allowances and the direction in which the final ones need to be pressed.

Once you have joined the 4 blocks of each corner, sew the top 2 units together, then the bottom 2 units. Next, join the 2 halves, and press. You should have found that every seam was pressed the correct direction to automatically butt properly. Planning the pressing every step of the way makes the final construction a breeze!

border information for this quilt
The inner border for this quilt is dark green and is ⅞″ wide, finished. The outer border is cut from the light green fabric and is 5″ wide, finished.

If you are interested in making the *Asian Nights* version, following are the yardages and blocks needed. The grid size and block size are the same as for *Town Square*, above.

Quilt top size: 48″ × 64″ (without borders)

Grid size: 1″

Layout: 8 rows of 6 blocks each

Blocks:

24 Block A

24 Block B

Yardage needed:

⅔ yard blue fabric

1¼ yards tan fabric

1¼ yards medium brown fabric

1 yard dark brown fabric

Asian Nights

border information for this quilt
The small inner border is cut from the blue fabric and is 1″ wide, finished, and the outer border is cut from the dark brown fabric and is 4¾″ wide, finished.

Wow! You have just completed a stunning quilt top that appears much more difficult than it actually was. Your new skills prepare you to make the quilts in Class 160.

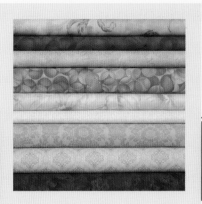

Class 160

For a quiltmaker, fabric and color become a love affair. Quilters tend to buy fabric impulsively. There is something about the color, texture, and feel of fabric that lures us into this art in the first place. So building a collection is no problem. In order to have a great collection, you need to have a wide variety of colors and prints.

How do you go about collecting fabric? You begin by understanding that different fabrics fall into different categories and that you need a combination of fabrics from these various categories. This basic knowledge will make fabric collecting much less intimidating and will help you determine whether your collection is a full-spectrum, balanced collection.

LESSON ONE:
Fabric collecting basics

Let's start out by looking at the categories fabrics fall into and what their effect can be on a quilt.

TYPES OF FABRICS

SOLIDS

Solid fabrics have no design or markings printed on them. With solids, you can create a very clean, contemporary look or a very traditional look like that of Amish quilts. Solids define and accentuate the print fabrics they are next to in the quilt design. However, solids do show every piecing flaw and uneven quilting stitch, so if you are a beginner, you may want to avoid working with a large amount of solid fabric in the beginning.

Solid fabrics

NEUTRALS

Neutrals are the beiges, tans, creams, grays, browns, and blacks. These colors will not change other colors, but they can add richness and compatibility to color schemes that seem to fight. This is a color group that you can never have enough of. These colors aren't exciting to buy, but they will enhance every one of your quilts.

Blender and neutral fabrics

SMALL PRINTS

Small-print fabrics usually have a small and subtle print of two contrasting colors. These fabrics tend to look like a solid from a distance but will add the texture that solids lack. This category of fabrics makes excellent backgrounds for piecing designs that have a very definite pattern to them.

Small prints

TONALS

Also known as *tone-on-tone* fabrics, these fabrics are printed within the same color family, usually with a lighter background and a darker print, or a mottled effect of several shades. An example would be a fabric that uses three different blues to create a floral pattern on a lighter blue background.

Tonals

CALICOES

Calico prints are fabrics with small prints that have one color for the background and two or more colors in the print design. Because of the various colors and sizes of the prints, be sure to stand back from the fabric and see which colors are predominant. In some calicoes, the background will be the only color you see from a distance, while in others, one or more colors from the print will stand out. Use calicoes in limited quantity in your quilts because they can look very "busy," and they don't give your eye a place to rest or the ability to take in the overall design of the quilt.

Calicoes

DOTS

Dots are fabrics with a one-color background and a dot or a print that looks like a dot from a distance, such as a print with flowers or apples. Your eyes tend to jump around when trying to focus on these fabrics. Dots can add interest, but, as with calicoes, too many can become very busy and detract from the design of the quilt. The fewer the fabrics your quilt design has, the more important it becomes to limit the use of this type of print.

VINY PRINTS

Viny prints tend to be larger in scale than small prints, with meandering lines running throughout. They have one background color and at least one other contrasting color used in the print. These prints read as airy and light, and add a lot of interest to the patchwork.

LARGE PRINTS

Large prints are prints with large patterns—usually of multiple colors—that can be splashy or subtle. Large prints offer many possibilities. When cut into pieces, they create movement and a variety of color combinations. Kept as a whole piece for a large square in a design, a large print becomes the focus fabric that everything else in the quilt works around.

Dots

Viny prints

Large prints

STRIPES

Striped fabrics contain bands of print or lines that most often run parallel to the selvage. They can be simple two-color stripes or multicolored, intricately patterned stripes. Stripes are exciting when used as borders or sashing.

Stripes

Color wheel

PLAIDS

Plaids are fabrics with lines—either woven or printed on the surface—that run perpendicular to each other. As with stripes, if it is important that the lines of the plaid be straight with a pattern, as in borders, sashing, and alternate blocks, then be advised that printed plaids (or stripes) are frequently printed off-grain, making them difficult to work with. Both plaids and stripes that are not straight are okay for use in pieced blocks, as long as having the lines of the print askew with the piecing does not distract your eye from the design of the quilt. These fabrics can add more interest to your quilts.

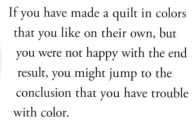

Plaids

DESIGN ELEMENTS

COLOR

If you have made a quilt in colors that you like on their own, but you were not happy with the end result, you might jump to the conclusion that you have trouble with color.

The first thing to do is to figure out what bothers you about the quilt. Perhaps it is too washed out, or the opposite—too high-contrast. Maybe there are too many busy prints or too many of the same scale or size of prints. Not everyone likes the same kind of feeling in a quilt, so don't ask someone else how to fix the problem until you know what the problem is *for you*.

First and foremost, it is important to know that, like beauty, color is very much in the eye of the beholder and is a matter of personal taste. If you like a particular color combination, then it is okay to use it! Color theory classes can be helpful, but just as often we have found that trying to pick fabric for a quilt based on artificial rules of the "proper use of color" only makes you afraid to trust your instincts about what you do and don't like. *All* colors go together!

There are four basic color schemes to keep in mind:

❋ Monochromatic (all one color)

❋ Complementary (colors that are across from one another on the color wheel)

❋ Analogous (colors that are next to one another on the color wheel)

❋ Polychromatic (all colors)

Every possible combination of colors fits somewhere into one of these color schemes. So relax! Trust your instincts and personal taste when selecting various colors to put together in your quilts.

VALUE

Value is the lightness or darkness of a color. The pure color from the color wheel is made lighter by adding white (a tint) or darker by adding black (a shade). Value is relative! The color, as well as the value, of a fabric will change according to the type of print, adjacent colors and objects, the light source and its position, the finish of the fabric, and so on.

All fabrics have their place on the light/dark scale. An example would be placing a medium green between a pale yellow and pale pink. The green would look quite dark in comparison. The same medium green placed between a dark navy and a burgundy would appear light. Fabrics of the same value will combine and run together when placed next to each other. An understanding of value will keep you from creating quilts that lack depth and interest.

Light to dark

Fabrics of the same value

Value is relative to placement

Value is relative to placement

INTENSITY

Intensity is the brightness factor of a color. A color can range from very dull to very bright. The pure color from the color wheel is the most intense it can be. The intensity of a color is changed when gray is added. The more gray you add, the duller the color appears.

It is really not important to know whether a certain piece of fabric is light or dark, dull or bright, unless that fabric is causing your quilt to look like it is missing something.

Range of color intensity

BECOMING FAMILIAR WITH FABRICS

So, how do you really begin to learn about fabrics and color? Our best suggestion is to visit your local quilt shop and just spend some time playing with combinations of fabrics. To learn about the different categories of prints, walk among the shelves and displays and start to identify the small prints, calicoes, viny and large prints, plaids, and stripes.

To learn about value and intensity, stack up combinations of fabrics and see what happens when you put something you may consider a medium with two lighter fabrics or two darker fabrics. A crutch you can use for determining value is a *value finder*, which can be a red see-through plastic report cover from a stationery store, or a tool such as a Ruby Beholder (available at quilt shops). When you look at a stack of fabrics through the value finder, you will immediately have a sense of whether a fabric is lighter or darker than others in the stack. The colors of the fabrics in the stack make no difference; what comes across is which of the fabrics are darker and which are lighter.

Value finder tools

Determining light, medium, and dark with a value finder

Most of all, remember that color choice is a personal preference. You may love a combination of colors and prints, only to have a salesclerk or friend try to discourage you and replace your choices with their preferences. Remember, this is your quilt and it must suit your likes and tastes. The more quilts you make, the more you'll learn about your personal preferences.

LESSON TWO:
Choosing fabrics for a quilt

Let us reassure you that a stash is not *necessary*, especially if you are a beginner. You may not know right now what colors you prefer. Perhaps, like Carrie, you may be very eclectic in your tastes, and you want to make a quilt with whatever fabric calls to you at the time. If you are feeling over-whelmed, we suggest that you simply buy the fabric you need as you come upon a quilt you want to make.

However, if you don't have a stash and are interested in building one, here's a good place to start: When you fall in love with a fabric for a particular quilt, buy the yardage you need for that quilt plus an extra ½ yard or more that will go into your stash. It may take you a while to build a usable stash this way, but it may also be the most economical way to do it.

Eclectic in your tastes or not, you may not find you need to possess a bunch of fabric, because again, if you are like Carrie, you just don't make the "scrappy" kinds of quilts that stashes lend themselves to. Harriet, in contrast, loves antique reproduction fabric. Because of its limited avail-ability, her stash is entirely comprised of fabric pieces ½ to 1 yard (or larger) in size that were available for only a very short time but that may be the perfect fabric in the next antique quilt she wants to reproduce.

No matter what your working style, or how you plan to go about quilting, you will need to choose fabrics for the quilts you want to make. Following is a list of suggestions to keep in mind

when you are choosing fabrics for your next project.

❋ **Start by falling in love with one fabric.** You might find it easier if this is a multicolored print of medium to large scale. Other fabrics can be chosen that have the colors used in the print of this one "focus" fabric. Make sure that if the large print is taken away, the other fabrics still work together and can stand on their own.

❋ **Choose prints that vary in scale.** The use of many different types and scales of prints will make the quilt come to life! If only tiny prints are used, they will cancel each other out, and the quilt will "die." If you select all large prints, the quilt will become extremely busy.

❋ **Use small prints and tiny dot-type fabrics instead of solids to create interest.**

❋ **Use small prints and tonals as blenders.** These subtle fabrics work as mortar to hold the units together. They are most often used as backgrounds in quilts because they don't compete and they allow the more interesting fabrics to look their best. Blenders also allow the design or pattern to be dominant.

❋ **Vary the theme of the print.** Too much of one pattern is not a good thing. Too many paisleys, rosebuds, or leaves—no matter the scales of the prints—will become monotonous.

❋ **Don't just work within a line of fabric your local store may have on display.** Branch out, and check for other fabrics on the shelves that may blend or add a spark to the focus fabric.

❋ **Choose the darker fabrics first and lighter fabrics last.** Medium and dark fabrics are easier to select. There are also more of them available than there are lights.

✻ **Satisfy the quilt before the room it is to live in or the person it is to live with.** Too many times, we overcoordinate a quilt to make it match wallpaper or carpeting, or to please the person to whom we plan on gifting the quilt, often to the detriment of the quilt. Let the quilt be a blending of the elements of the room it is to go in, instead of the showpiece. Instead of making the quilt in the recipient's favorite color, use many shades of the colors he or she likes.

✻ **Experiment with fabrics that may "clash" a bit.** Clashing is not always bad. It keeps a quilt from being ho-hum. Instead of rust, try maroon. Instead of navy, try purple or mauve. Try a color that looks good with the whole quilt.

✻ **Don't be afraid to throw in a little black.** Black will put life into colors and give them spark.

✻ **Think about what you like the most.** Think about the colors you tend to prefer. Become aware of color in your environment. Advertisements, greeting cards, upholstery color schemes, flower gardens, and so forth offer great inspiration. Clip out ideas from magazines, and make notes of color combinations you see and like.

✻ **Three, five, or seven fabrics are good numbers to aim for when you begin to make quilts.** Scrap quilts made of many fabrics can be overwhelming when you are first starting out.

✻ **Pull the fabric off the quilt shop shelf and look at it alone and in the light.** Other fabrics on the shelf, as well as shadows from the shelf itself, can affect the color of the fabric.

✻ **Stack the selected bolts; then step back six to ten feet, and squint at them.** This will help the colors stand out, and you'll notice which colors are too similar or too bold, or blend too much. Squinting magnifies the differences between the fabrics. After some trial and error, you'll develop a combination that includes dark, light, and medium, as well as varying print scales. If you squint at them, and they live harmoniously together, you probably have a winner!

✻ **Lay the bolts on their sides so that you are seeing only the edges of the bolts.** Remember that you'll be cutting the fabric into small pieces. Seeing the fabrics in the relationship and proportion in which they will appear in the block can prove quite helpful.

✻ **Go with your instincts.** If you feel that a combination looks too busy, it probably is. If the colors make you nervous, don't use them. You need to like your fabric, but remember that trial and error and experimentation are your best ways to learn. (Carrie made two different quilts for this book in which fabrics that looked great when they were selected just didn't look right when pieced. One looked too busy, and in the other the colors just didn't work.) Your tastes will change, but you must be willing to take a chance occasionally.

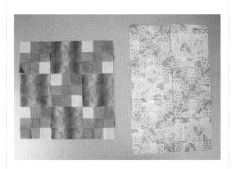

Carrie's "missed" quilts

✻ **Intense or contrasting colors can emphasize parts of a design.** Conversely, a low-contrast combination can give the eye a place to rest.

✻ **Be aware of one-way prints.** They have a distinct up and down direction and can appear upside down if not placed carefully. Toiles are a very good example of one-way print fabrics.

✻ **Utilize the "view-a-patch" system.** Cut various template shapes and sizes from a sheet of frosted or white template plastic. Place one on the fabric to see how it will look when cut up. You can precut templates.

"View-a-patch" tools

✻ **Among the following: type and scale of print, value and intensity, and color, you will find that color is the least important.** If your fabric selections are strong on color but weak on the other two elements, you can end up with a very boring quilt!

✻ **Look at the fabric in natural light if possible.** Artificial lighting can distort colors and the way they relate to each other. When making a quilt for a specific place, we suggest that you also look at the fabrics in that environment to see how the colors work together.

LESSON THREE:
Constructing perfect Nine-Patch blocks

In this lesson, you will be making twelve Nine-Patch blocks for the sampler quilt you have started. Nine-Patch blocks are not that different from Four-Patch blocks, but each square within the block tends to be smaller, and there is more sewing and butting seams involved. Nine-Patch blocks are made of three rows of three squares each.

✳ EXERCISE: CONSTRUCTING NINE-PATCH BLOCKS FOR THE SAMPLER QUILT

Materials:

Dark and light fabrics from Exercise: Sampler quilt blocks (page 27), in which you made the Fence Post and Four-Patch blocks

There are 2 different strip sets needed for Nine-Patch blocks. Rows 1 and 3 are the same, and Row 2 is the negative of 1 and 3, creating a checkerboard.

Color placement for strip sets

This block uses a 1″ grid. Many beginners are told that small grids are difficult, and the common theory is to teach beginners with large-scale grids. Harriet has found that her students love the detail and repeat of small grids, and that 1″ is not difficult—it

just takes more blocks to fill the space needed. We hope you enjoy making 3″ Nine-Patch blocks. Remember, accuracy is critical.

1. To figure out how many strip sets you need to make the 12 blocks, count how many segments you need for the blocks for Rows 1 and 3. There are 2 segments in each block, so 2 × 12 blocks = 24 segments. The cut size of each is 1½″, so 24 × 1.5″ = 36″ needed. That is 1 set of strips, cut the width of the fabric. Row 2 is only 1 cut per block (1 × 12 = 12 × 1.5″ = 18″ needed). That's about a ½ strip set.

Cut:

3 strips 1½″ wide of the solid blue fabric

2 strips 1½″ wide of the blue print fabric

2. Stitch a long blue and a blue print strip together, keeping the edges of the strips perfectly aligned. Press toward the blue strip and starch lightly. Measure from the seam to each raw edge, and check that the measurement is exactly 1¼″. If it isn't, either trim or check the seam allowance for accurate sewing.

3. Add another long blue strip to the blue print side, and stitch, aligning the edges exactly. Press toward the blue strip, and check that it is now 1¼″ wide.

4. Repeat Steps 2 and 3 for Row 2, reversing the color of the strips, still pressing toward the blue strip.

5. Cut the strips into segments, each 1½″ wide. You now have 2 seams to align the ruler. Lay the strip set on the mat horizontally. Trim the ends off the strip set on the right end (left end if you are left-handed). Turn the strip around 180°, lay the 1½″ ruler line on the cut end, and align the horizontal

ruler lines with the seamlines. Cut. Keep cutting 1½″ segments, keeping an eye on all the lines of the ruler.

Cutting strips into 1½″ segments

6. After a few cuts, you might find that the cut edge is not square with the seamlines. Turn the strip around and resquare the end, then resume cutting segments. You know from the figuring above that you need to cut 24 dark-light-dark segments and 12 light-dark-light segments.

7. Divide the segments into 3 stacks: 12 of Rows 1 and 3, 12 of Row 2, and 12 of Rows 1 and 3 again.

Stacks of nine-patch segments

8. Sew all 12 of Row 1 to Row 2. Fan the seam intersections, and press. Starch lightly. Check the width of each side of the seam to be sure it is 1¼″.

9. Add Row 3. Fan the seams, and press. Starch lightly again. Check the measurement. Your Nine-Patch blocks should be exactly 3½″ square.

Back of block showing fanned seams

LESSON FOUR:
Continuing with precision piecing

In this lesson, you will build on your piecing skills to make interesting quilts that use Nine-Patch blocks in different, creative ways.

PROJECT: CARRIE'S *INTERLACING CIRCLES* QUILT

Quilt top size: 27″ × 27″ (without borders)

Grid size of smallest unit: 1¼″

Block size: 3¾″ × 3¾″

Blocks:

16 Nine-Patch blocks (Block A)

16 Rail Fence blocks (Block B), Color Set 1

8 Rail Fence blocks (Block C), Color Set 2

5 solid red squares

4 light print squares

Layout: 7 rows of 7 blocks each

Yardage requirements:

⅝ yard cream print fabric

⅓ yard dark red fabric

¼ yard red paisley fabric

¼ yard dark pink fabric

¼ yard dark red fabric for inner border

⅝ yard cream print fabric for outer border

This complex-looking quilt is made up of 3 different blocks: 3-color Nine-Patch blocks, Rail Fence blocks in 2 different color sets, and solid squares

Interlacing Circles

arranged to create an "interlacing circle" appearance.

MAKING THE NINE-PATCH BLOCKS

As with all your quilts, you will make the block with the most seams or the smallest grid first. Here, that's the Nine-Patch block. These blocks, unlike the ones you made for the sampler quilt, are made from 3 different strip sets.

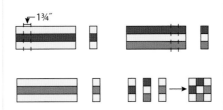

Nine-Patch strip sets and color placement for finished block

You will need 1 segment of each strip set to make each of the 16 Nine-Patch blocks. Each segment is cut 1¾″ wide, so 16 × 1.75″ = 28″, or 1 strip of each fabric for each strip set. This means you need to cut 2 strips of the dark red and the red paisley, and 5 strips of the cream print.

1. Sew together the first 2 strips of each of the strip sets. Press the seam allowance toward the dark fabric (either the red or the paisley), and starch. Check strip width accuracy, and trim down to 1½″ if necessary.

2. Sew the third strip onto each set, and again press, measure, and trim if needed.

3. Cut each strip set into 16 segments 1¾" wide. Place the stacks of the 3 strip sets to the right of your machine. Pick up a cream-red-cream segment (1) in your left hand, and a red-cream-paisley segment (2) in your right. Put 2 on top of 1, right sides together, butt the seams, and sew. Repeat until all the segments in the 2 stacks are sewn together.

4. Until now, you have been fanning the seams for both Four-Patches and Nine-Patches. In this quilt you cannot fan the seams because they will only butt up properly half the time with the Rail Fence blocks they are sewn to. So, when you press the first construction seams of the Nine-Patches, you will be pressing the seams toward the red-cream-paisley segments. Press and starch, and again check for accuracy of width, and trim if necessary.

5. Add the last segments to the Nine-Patch. These segments are to be sewn onto the red-cream-paisley side of the block. Butt the seams, and sew. At the ironing board, you will press this new seam toward the red-cream-paisley segment, and starch. Check for strip width accuracy. The blocks should all measure 4¼". Set these aside.

MAKING THE RAIL FENCE BLOCKS

The Rail Fence blocks in this quilt have 2 different color combinations, and so you need to make 2 different strip sets, as shown.

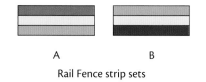

A   B

Rail Fence strip sets

You will need 16 blocks from Strip Set A and 8 blocks from Strip Set B. The rail blocks will be cut 4¼" wide, so for the Strip Set A blocks: 16 × 4.25" = 68", and 68" ÷ 42" fabric width = 1.6, or 2 strips of each color (paisley, cream, and dark pink). For the 8 blocks from Strip Set B: 8 × 4.25" = 34", or 1 strip of each color (dark pink, cream, and red). Cut 3 strips of the dark pink and cream, 2 strips of the paisley, and 1 strip of the red.

1. Sew these strip sets together just like you did for all the other Rail Fence blocks you have made thus far. Press the seam allowances toward the dark colors in the strip sets. Don't forget to measure and check the strips for width every time you sew a seam—they should measure 1½".

2. Once you have all 3 strips sewn together, the middle strip should measure 1¼" wide. Cut the strips into 4¼" blocks. Set aside. You're almost finished!

MAKING THE SOLID SQUARES

You need 5 red and 4 cream squares. They all measure 4¼" square. For the red, 5 × 4.25" = 21.25". For the cream, 4 × 4.25" = 17". So, you need 1 strip for each.

Cut the strips 4¼" wide, then cut them into squares.

ASSEMBLING THE QUILT TOP

Referring to the layout diagram, lay out the quilt top. Be careful to turn those Nine-Patch blocks the right way to create the circle patterns!

Layout for *Interlacing Circles*

1. Place all the blocks in each row into stacks, as described in Class 130 (pages 29–30), and take the complete quilt top to the sewing machine at one time. You will have 7 stacks of 7 blocks each beside your machine.

2. Construct all the rows. Press the seam allowances toward the Rail Fence blocks. Because this block appears in every other spot, the seams will be ready to butt properly.

3. Once the blocks are joined into rows and the rows are joined, set the quilt top aside. You will add borders when you get to Class 180.

border information for this quilt

The inner border for this quilt is cut from the red fabric; it is 1½" wide, finished. The outer border is cut from the cream fabric; it is 5" wide, finished.

PROJECT: HARRIET'S *DOUBLE NINE-PATCH CHAIN* QUILT

Quilt top size: 45″ × 45″

(without borders)

Grid size of smallest unit: 1″

Block size: 9″ × 9″

Blocks:

12 Block A (Chain block)

13 Block B (Nine-Patch block)

Layout: 5 rows of 5 blocks each

Yardages for quilt top:

⅓ yard blue fabric

⅔ yard large-print fabric

1½ yards tan fabric

1 yard large-print fabric for border

note *Just a reminder that the yardages are the minimum you need. Remember to add enough for your comfort level in case of cutting errors, or if you need extra for straightening the grain (if the fabric was cut from the bolt).*

This is a quilt of Nine-Patch blocks, and a Nine-Patch block made of nine-patches! However, if you look closely, the corners of the Chain block are different from a standard Nine-Patch. We are combining 2 grids to cut 1 wider piece to fill the place of 2 smaller pieces. Since the grid is 1″, the wider space equals 2″ plus the seam allowances.

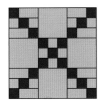

Chain block

Double Nine-Patch Chain

MAKING THE CHAIN BLOCK (BLOCK A)

1. Start by making the nine-patch units in the center of the block. How many strip sets are needed to accommodate 12 blocks?

Rows 1 and 3: 2 segments for each block × 1½″ cut = 3″ × 12 blocks = 36″, or 1 strip set

Row 2: 1 segment for each block × 1½″ cut = 1½″ × 12 blocks = 18″, or ½ strip set

You need 2 strips of blue for Rows 1 and 3, and ½ strip for Row 2 (you will have to cut a full strip). You need 1 strip of tan for Rows 1 and 3, and 1 strip for Row 2.

Cut:

3 strips of the blue fabric (1 cut in half)

2 strips of the tan fabric (1 cut in half)

Lay out the strips as follows:

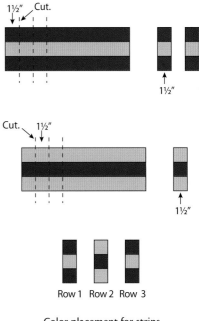

Row 1 Row 2 Row 3

Color placement for strips

2. Construct strip sets as you have learned in this class, checking the width of each strip after each addition. Press, starch, and cut the strip sets into 1½″ segments. Build stacks of 12 segments for each row. Stitch together Row 1 and Row 2. Fan the seams, and press. Add Row 3. Fan the seams, and press. Measure to be sure that each block is exactly 3½″ square.

3. Make the corner blocks next. They are a bit different from a true Nine-Patch. Because of the chain that runs through the block, the 2 sides are mirror images of each other. Therefore, you will need to be careful to make them separately and lay out the small blocks carefully when constructing the large Chain block.

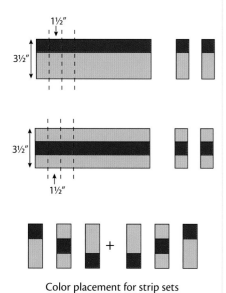

Corner blocks

4. Again you will need 2 strip sets. All the strip sets can be made at the same time, but when you get ready to build the blocks, the layout will be different.

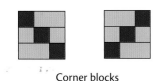

Color placement for strip sets

5. These strip sets are again cut into 1½″ segments. You need 4 modified Nine-Patch blocks for each large block, and there are 12 large blocks, for a total of 48 blocks you need to make.

6. Rows 1 and 3 are the same. You need 2 segments for each block: $2 \times 4 = 8 \times 1.5″ = 12″ \times 12$ blocks $= 144″ \div 42″ = 3.43$, or 4 strip sets. Row 2 is the same as Row 2 of the center nine-patch we made on page 78: $1 \times 4 = 4 \times 1.5″ = 6″ \times 12 = 72″ \div 42″ = 1.71$, or 2 strip sets. (All these strip sets could be made at the same time.)

Cut:

4 strips 1½″ wide of the blue fabric

4 strips 2½″ wide of the tan fabric

2 strips 1½″ wide of the blue fabric

4 strips 1½″ wide of the tan fabric

7. Construct these strip sets, press, starch, and measure for accuracy with each addition of a strip. Cut into segments. You will need 96 segments for Rows 1 and 3, and 48 segments for Row 2.

8. Before making the stacks for chain sewing, divide the segments in half. Because the position of the wide strip is mirrored from side to side, the blocks have different layouts.

Top left /   Top right /
bottom right block   bottom left block

Lay out the rows for the left blocks into stacks, and chain sew Rows 1 and 2. After fanning the seams and pressing, add Row 3. Repeat for the right blocks.

9. Now add the solid squares to the Chain blocks. Because of their size and the tricky layout of the corner blocks, it is smart to precut the squares and lay out the large block in rows. All the rows can be joined together as we have been doing, and the direction of the corner blocks can be checked during the process. Lay out the units of the large block as shown below.

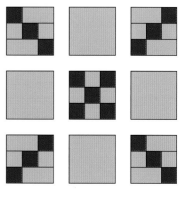

Block layout

10. Gather up each row and stack the blocks as before. You will have 12 units in each stack. Begin sewing by stitching the first 2 blocks of Row 1 together, 2 on top of 1. Press the seams toward the large square. Add the third block of the row. Again, press toward the large square. Repeat for Rows 2 and 3. Once the rows are finished, sew Row 1 to Row 2. Press toward Row 2. Add Row 3. Press toward Row 2 again. Starch the blocks to make sure all the seams are flat and well pressed.

11. Again, check the size and squareness of the blocks. Using a 4½″ ruler, place the 3¼″ line on a seam and check that the raw edge is exactly 3¼″. Do this to all 4 sides of all 12 blocks. The blocks must measure exactly 9½″, with the blue corner squares measuring 1¼″.

MAKING THE LARGE NINE-PATCH BLOCK (BLOCK B)

Nine-Patch block

1. Again, for each block 2 strip sets are needed. How many strip sets do you need? There are 13 blocks. Each row needs 3½" for each segment. Two segments are needed per block for Rows 1 and 3, and 1 segment for Row 2.

Rows 1 and 3: 2 × 3.5" = 7" × 13 blocks = 91" ÷ 42" = 2.16, or about 2½ strip sets.

Row 2: 1 × 3.5" = 3.5" × 13 blocks = 45.5, or a bit more than 1 strip set. You can figure 1½ strip sets.

For both strip sets, cut:

7 strips 3½" wide of the large-print fabric

6 strips 3½" wide of the tan fabric

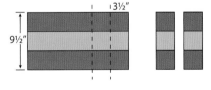

Rows 1 and 3

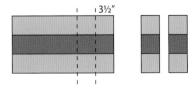

Row 2

Color placement for strip sets

2. For Rows 1 and 3, sew 2½ strips of large print to 2½ strips of tan. Press each set of strips toward the large print. Measure both sides of the seam to check that the strips are now exactly 3¼" wide. Add another large-print strip to the tan of each strip set. Press toward the large print again. Check that this strip is now exactly 3¼" wide. Cut the strips into segments. You will need 26 segments 3½" wide.

3. For Row 2, sew 1½ strips of tan to large-print strips. Press toward the large print. Check that each strip is now 3¼" wide. Add another tan strip to the large-print sides. Press and check for width accuracy. Cut these strip sets into 13 segments 3½" wide.

4. Lay out the segments to form the block shown. There must be 13 segments in each stack. Start constructing the block by sewing the 13 Row 1 segments to the 13 Row 2 segments, carefully butting the seams. Press this seam toward Row 1. Do not fan the seams in this block. Add the 13 segments for Row 3 to Row 2. Press this seam toward Row 3.

5. To check for accuracy, measure off each seam to the outside edge. Make sure each side is exactly 3¼" wide from the seam.

6. You are now ready to lay out the blocks. The A and B blocks alternate, starting with the large Nine-Patch Block B in the top left corner. There are 5 blocks in each row, and 5 rows in the quilt top.

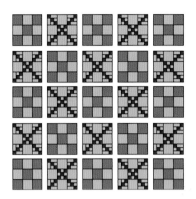

Double Nine-Patch Chain layout

7. As before, begin stacking up the rows with the first block on the left as #1, on top of 2, 3, 4, and finally 5. Mark the block to denote the top. Repeat with the next 4 rows. Lay these stacks beside your machine, and begin sewing by sewing the first 2 blocks of all the rows together. The seams should butt perfectly because of the direction the rows were pressed within each block. Press the seams toward the large Nine-Patch block. When all the rows are connected, roll Row 1 over Row 2, and sew the long seam, butting the seams exactly. Press in either direction. Continue until all 5 rows have been joined.

border information for this quilt

There is only a single border on this quilt that finishes to be 6" wide.

Set your finished quilt top aside. In Class 180, you will learn how to check for square corners and accuracy of width and length, and how to add borders.

Class 170

One of the most useful things that you can learn right from the beginning is how to calculate yardage for your projects. When you figure your own yardage, you have the assurance that you have enough fabric to complete the project without having too much left over. Often patterns load up the yardage, and you buy more than you need. At today's prices, this can really cut into your fabric budget. You will also find that as you figure the yardage, you can make your own "recipe" for the cutting and construction of the blocks. This will help you work more efficiently and confidently.

As you work through this class, you will learn to figure the yardage needed for the blocks, borders, and backing of your projects.

note Important: Always figure yardage using cut sizes!

LESSON ONE:
Understanding terminology

The fabric produced for quilting today is generally 44″–45″ wide. Once you take off the selvages and allow for possible shrinkage if you choose to prewash, consider the usable width of the fabric to be 40″–42″ wide.

note If you prewash your fabric, we suggest that you check the width after drying. If your fabric is less than 42 usable inches, use your measurement instead of 42″ when working through the exercises throughout this book.

As you study your quilt design, determine whether you'll be cutting strips for the project, and if so, whether you will cut them across the width (crosswise) or along the selvage edge (lengthwise) of the fabric. If the strips are cut crosswise, the strip measurement will be 42″. If you choose to cut the strips lengthwise, the measurement can vary with the length of fabric available, so the strip length measurement will need to be determined.

For the following examples we will be working with 42" strips.

Once you begin to think in terms of strips, squares, rectangles, and other shapes, figuring yardage is greatly simplified. In a quilt made only with strips, everything is being cut from strips. Once you know how long the strips will be, think of how many units you can obtain from each strip, and thus how many strips are needed to produce the required number of units for the quilt. When a quilt contains blocks with several different shapes, you need to identify every different shape, size, and color planned for the quilt, and how they can be cut from strips to simplify figuring yardage.

Reading the blocks

There are a few givens when figuring yardage. When figuring the sequence of the strips to be sewn together, we read across the top of the block. This also tells us the cut width of each strip. Running inches of each unit are read down the side of the block. This tells us how long each segment is cut from the strip set. For the following examples, the running length of each strip will be figured on 42".

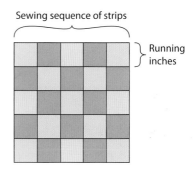

Sewing sequence of strips

Running inches

Reading the block for measurements

LESSON THREE:
Working through the
Double Irish Chain baby quilt

You will be making this baby quilt in this class, so it's a good example to use in learning to figure yardage. This quilt has 2 different blocks: 18 of Block A and 17 of Block B. To figure the yardage, let's look at how the formula works. *Remember to always use cut sizes when figuring yardage.*

The blocks in this quilt will be a 1″ grid, making the cut size of each square 1½″. This is a five-patch block, so the blocks will finish out to 5″. Let's start with **Block A** to work through the formula.

BLOCK A

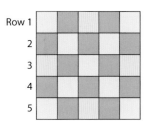

Block A

Step 1: Count the total number of like units.

In this block, there are 3 different units. Each color square in the block—pink, blue, and white—is a different unit. There are:

9 blue units

12 pink units

4 white units

Step 2: Multiply that number by their cut length.

Do this for each different color, shape, and unit's position in that block.

For the example, when you read the side of the block, you know that the

squares are finished to 1″, so the cut size is 1.5″.

9 blue units × 1.5″ = 13.5″

12 pink units × 1.5″ = 18″

4 white units × 1.5″ = 6″

Step 3: Multiply this number by the total number of like blocks.

Refer to the photo of the quilt and count the number of blocks that look like Block A. There are 18. You need 13.5″ of pink from a strip for 1 block. You need to make 18 of Block A.

Blue: 13.5″ for 1 block × 18 = 243″

Pink: 18″ for 1 block × 18 = 324″

White: 6″ for 1 block × 18 = 108″

Step 4: Divide this number by 42″.

This will give you the number of strips needed of that color, for the unit of that block. If you are using a

different strip length, use that measurement instead of 42″. (Round this number up if it's a fraction.)

Blue: 243″ ÷ 42″ = 5.79, rounded up to 6 strips

Pink: 324″ ÷ 42″ = 7.71, rounded up to 8 strips

White: 108″ ÷ 42″ = 2.57, rounded up to 3 strips

Step 5: Multiply this number by the cut width of the strip.

This measurement is determined by reading across the top of the block or row. In this case, because all the units are square, you know that the width is the same as the length: 1.5″.

Blue: 6 strips × 1.5″ = 9″ needed

Pink: 8 strips × 1.5″ = 12″ needed

White: 3 strips × 1.5″ = 4.5″ needed

Double Irish Chain baby quilt

The above answers tell you how much fabric you need to buy to accommodate Block A throughout the quilt. Do not convert it into yardage cuts yet, as we will have more to add to it as we work through the second block.

BLOCK B

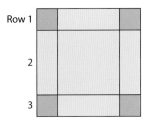

Block B

Using the Formula again, let's determine the needed fabric for Block B.

Step 1: Count the total number of like units.

There are 4 different *like units* in this block. Unlike Block A, in which all the units are the same shape and size, Block B has combined grids on the top and bottom of the block as well as along the sides of the block, and it has a center square, totaling 4 different units. The long pieces on the top and bottom are not the same as the sides. The top and bottom units are wide and short, and the side units are long and narrow. This is one of the most confusing aspects of identifying shapes and position, but it must be considered if the yardage is to be accurate.

Pink: 4 units

White: 2 top and bottom units

    2 side units

    1 center square

Step 2: Multiply that number by their cut length.

Do this for each different color, shape, and unit's position in that block.

Pink: 4 units × 1.5″ = 6″

White: 2 units × 1.5″ = 3″

White: 2 units × 3.5″ = 7″

White: 1 unit × 3.5″ = 3.5″

Step 3: Multiply this number by the total number of like blocks.

Refer to the photo of the quilt and count the number of blocks that look like Block B. You need 17 of Block B.

Pink: 6″ × 17 blocks = 102″

White: 3″ × 17 = 51″

White: 7″ × 17 = 119″

White: 3.5″ × 17 = 59.5″

Step 4: Divide this number by 42″.

Pink: 102″ ÷ 42″ = 2.43, rounded up to 3 strips

White: 51″ ÷ 42″ = 1.21, rounded up to 2 strips

White: 119″ ÷ 42″ = 2.83, rounded up to 3 strips

White: 59.5″ ÷ 42″ = 1.42, rounded up to 2 strips

tip If you come up with numbers like 2.02, quickly do the math: 0.02 × 42″ = 0.84″. If your fabric is actually a bit wider than 42″, numbers ranging from 0.01 to 0.05 are so small that one more unit could possibly be accommodated by the extra length, allowing for two strips instead of three. Check the size of the unit needed against the width of the fabric.

Step 5: Multiply this number by the cut width of the strip.

Pink: 3 strips × 1.5″ = 4.5″ needed

White: 2 strips × 3.5″ = 7″ needed

White: 3 strips × 1.5″ = 4.5″ needed

White: 2 strips × 3.5″ = 7″ needed

You now know how much fabric you will need to make all 35 blocks.

Blue: 9″ = ¼ yard (6 strips 1.5″ wide)

Pink: 12″ + 4.5″ = 16.5″ = ½ yard (11 strips 1.5″ wide)

White: 4.5″ + 7″ + 4.5″ + 7″ = 23″ = ⅔ yard (6 strips 1.5″ wide; 4 strips 3.5″ wide)

Yardage to decimals & inches

Fractions	Decimals	Inches
⅛	0.125	4½
¼	0.25	9
⅓	0.333	12
⅜	0.375	13½
½	0.5	18
⅝	0.625	22½
⅔	0.666	24
¾	0.75	27
⅞	0.875	32½
1	1	36

note As discussed in Class 120 (page 13), you must consider whether fabric is torn or cut from the bolt when you figure yardage. If the fabric has been cut, you might need to add up to ¼ yard to your final figures (beyond the ⅛ yard you added for safety when figuring strips needed), so that the ends can be torn and the fabric can be straightened before cutting.

note This method of figuring yardage is a continuous formula on a calculator and works quickly and simply for small grids and blocks with many units. As the blocks become larger in later books, we will add methods that are appropriate at the time.

Combined grids

Following are your first *combined grid* quilts. As explained in Reading the Blocks (page 81) and in Class 150, where you learned about drafting, a combined grid is a design in which 1 or more parts of the design are a solid piece that is 2 or more times the size of the grid.

PROJECT: CARRIE'S *INLAID TILE* TABLE RUNNER

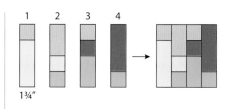

Inlaid Tile table runner

Quilt top size: 15″ × 60″ (without borders)

Grid size of smallest unit: 1¼″

Block size: 5″ × 5″

Blocks: 36

Layout: 3 rows of 12 blocks each

Yardage requirements:

⅜ yard yellow fabric

⅜ yard green fabric

⅜ yard light blue fabric

⅜ yard dark blue fabric

2 yards border strip (Note: This is if the border strip runs parallel to the selvage and there are at least 3 repeats across the width of the fabric.)

For this quilt, you have only 1 type of block to construct. That 1 block is made from 4 different strip sets.

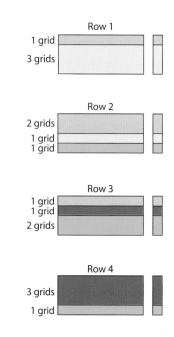

Row 1
1 grid
3 grids

Row 2
2 grids
1 grid
1 grid

Row 3
1 grid
1 grid
2 grids

Row 4
3 grids
1 grid

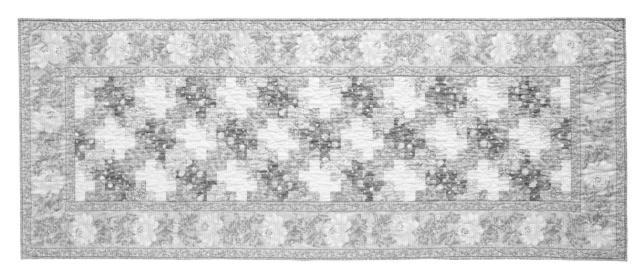

1   2   3   4

1¾″

Inlaid Tile strip sets

To make enough strip sets for 36 blocks, you need 36 segments 1¾″ wide. So, 36 × 1.75″ = 63″ ÷ 42″ = 1.5, or 2 strips of each. Before you precut all the strips to make the strip sets, let's focus for a moment on constructing combined grids. In order to have the parts of the block that are a combined grid come out to be the exact size, you will need to cut and construct the strips that are the size of the grid (the smallest) and then measure those for size. Then you will cut the next widest strip to that size and sew it, and so on, if you have multiple combined grids as this *Inlaid Tile* quilt does. Sound a little confusing? It really isn't, and it will make more sense as you do it, so off we go!

CONSTRUCTING THE STRIP SETS

Rows 2 and 3 have the most seams, so they must be made first, just as we did with the *Country Lanes* and *Interlacing Circles* quilts (pages 60 and 75). This way you can be sure that the mathematical measurements agree with your measurements after you sew the seams. If they are off, you can adjust the width the strips are cut if necessary to correct for any discrepancy when piecing the strip sets for Rows 1 and 4, which have fewer seams.

1. Cut the narrow strips for Rows 2 and 3 first. You need 2 strips 1¾" wide of each color—yellow, green, light blue, and dark blue. Lay out the strips so that they match the diagrams on page 84, and sew the 2 narrow strips of each strip set together.

2. Press the seam toward the green fabric for Row 2, and toward the light blue fabric for Row 3. At the cutting table, measure from the seamline to ensure that the strips are now 1½" wide, and trim if necessary.

3. Now you need 2 strips *each* of light blue and green, cut 3" wide. This is the first place where combined grids come into play. The measurement of the wide strip should be exactly the same as the measurement of the 2 narrow strips sewn together. If you were not accurate with your cutting or sewing, you can compensate for size discrepancy

by working from your unique measurements (YUMs). Sew the light blue fabric to the Row 2 strip sets, and the green fabric to the Row 3 strip sets. For Row 2, press this seam toward the light blue, and for Row 3, press toward the green. Again, measure from the seam allowance for strip width accuracy. This new wide strip should measure 2¾"; trim to this width if needed.

4. Turn the strip sets wrong side up. On all 4 of the strip sets, measure from the raw edge of the wide strip (light blue in Row 2, green in Row 3) to the raw edge of the first narrow strip to which the wide strip is sewn (yellow in Row 2, dark blue in Row 3).

5. If you come up with 4¼", go ahead and cut the strips for Rows 1 and 4. If your measurement is different (either smaller or larger), you will need to cut the 3-grid-wide strips in Rows 1 and 4 to the width of the measurement you came up with. For example, if your measurement comes up at 4⅛", then you will cut your wide strips of yellow and dark blue to 4⅛" wide instead of 4¼". This is "your unique measurement," or YUM.

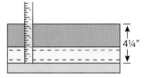

Measuring back side of strips to determine measurement for next strip

6. Now you're ready to sew the strip sets for Rows 1 and 4. We already figured that you need 2 strips of each fabric in each row to make 36 blocks. That means you need 2 strips 1¾" wide each of light blue and of green, and 2 strips 4¼" wide (or YUM) of yellow and of dark blue.

7. There is only 1 seam to sew for each row. Sew the strips together, and press the seam allowance toward the yellow for Row 1, and toward the dark blue for Row 4. Take these strip sets to your cutting mat and measure from the seam allowance to make sure that the strips are the correct size. If not, trim.

Making the blocks

1. From each of the strip sets, cut 36 segments 1¾″ wide. Place the stacks of segments to the right side of your sewing machine in the order shown on page 85: Row 1 on the left, then Row 2 to the right, Row 3 to the right of that, and Row 4 at the right end.

2. Sew Rows 2 and 3 together first, making sure that all the seams butt up perfectly. Before you press, fan the butted seams in the center of the block to help eliminate the bulkiness of all the seams coming together and to alleviate any distortion in the wide strips from the seam allowances being pressed onto them.

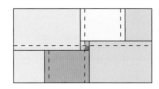

Fanning seam between Rows 2 and 3

3. Press the seam allowances in each direction, and starch lightly. Take these partial blocks to your cutting table, and measure from the seam allowance. Each of the row segments should measure 1½″. Trim off any excess.

4. Add Row 1 onto the Row 2 side of the block. Press the seam allowances open to reduce bulk, and starch and trim the Row 1 segment as before. Finally, add on the Row 4 segments, press the seam open, starch, and trim.

Assembling the quilt top

Layout time! This quilt can be a little bit of a brain bender until you have the first few blocks of Rows 1 and 2 established. We highly recommend that you build this quilt in sets of 4 blocks, making a square at a time so that you start to see the pattern develop. Once you see the pattern, it becomes much easier to flip the blocks the correct direction to keep the pattern going.

Use the quilt layout to the right as a guide. This layout is for a square quilt, 6 blocks wide by 6 blocks long. If you want to make a table runner like Carrie's, then refer to the photo at the beginning of this section. The table runner is 3 blocks wide by 12 blocks long. You are by no means restricted to just these 2 layouts. Play around with your blocks and see what happens if you make a wider, shorter table runner that is 4 blocks wide by 9 blocks long. Have fun with this one!

Square *Inlaid Tile* quilt layout

1. Once you have the quilt laid out the way you want it, repeat again what you learned in Class 130. Gather all the blocks in each row into stacks, and take the complete quilt to the machine. For the 6 × 6 quilt you will have 6 stacks of 6 blocks each beside your machine. If you are making the table runner, you will have 3 stacks of 12 blocks each. Or you will have stacks numbering whatever number of rows you have created, with the number of blocks in those piles equal to the number of blocks you have running across the width of the quilt. Start sewing.

2. Press all the seams of Row 1 to the right, all Row 2 seams to the left, all Row 3 seams to the right again, and so on, so that all the seams will butt when you join the rows together.

3. Once the blocks have been joined into rows and the rows have been joined, you are ready to add borders. Set the quilt top aside until you get to Class 180.

border information for this quilt

For the border of this quilt, Carrie chose a printed stripe that ran parallel to the selvage of the fabric. The corners are mitered so that the flowers trail around the corners of the quilt instead of dead-ending. Instructions for creating perfect mitered corners can be found in Class 180 (page 98). This border stripe finishes at 6½″ wide.

PROJECT: CARRIE'S *DOUBLE IRISH CHAIN* BABY QUILT

Quilt top size: 25¾″ × 35¾″ (without borders)

Grid size of smallest unit: 1″

Block size: 5″ × 5″

Blocks:

18 Block A

17 Block B

Layout: 7 rows of 5 blocks each

Yardage requirements:

⅓ yard blue fabric

½ yard pink fabric

¾ yard white fabric

The *Double Irish Chain* is a classic quilt pattern with timeless appeal. In the exercise for this class, you figured the yardage for this quilt (page 82), so we are going to dive right into constructing the blocks.

MAKING BLOCK A

For Rows 1 and 5, you need 3 strips of blue and of pink, and 1½ strips of white, all cut 1½″ wide.

For Rows 2 and 4, you need 3 strips of blue, 4½ strips of pink, and 3 strips of white, all cut 1½″ wide.

For Row 3, you need 1½ strips of blue, 3 strips of pink, and 3 strips of white, again all cut 1½″ wide.

Double Irish Chain baby quilt

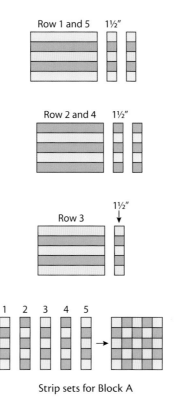

Strip sets for Block A

1. Cut the strips, lay them out in the order of the rows, and start sewing them together. For Rows 1 and 5, and Rows 2 and 4, you will have 1½ strip sets of each to sew together, and only 1 set for Row 3. Press all the seams for all the strip sets toward the pink. After you press, remember to trim the strips to the correct width. Each strip with 1 seam taken up will measure 1¼″ from the seam allowance.

2. Cut the strip sets into 1½″ segments. You need 36 of Rows 1, 2, 4, and 5 and only 18 of Row 3. Make stacks for each row from the strip sets.

3. To assemble Block A, transfer the stacks to the right side of your sewing machine. Start with Row 1 and Row 2 (2 on top of 1), butting the seams carefully. Chain sew the units.

4. Fan just the seam allowance for the white square (it should fold back on itself). Press the rest of the seam allowances on either side toward Row 2. Starch and trim.

Fanned seam for Block A, Rows 1 and 2

5. Add Row 3, and again fan just the seam of the middle block (the blue square) so that it folds back on itself and the rest of the seam folds onto Row 2 again. Press, starch, and trim.

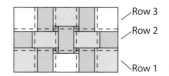

Fanned seam for Block A, Rows 1, 2, and 3

6. Add Row 4. Fan the middle pink block seam toward Row 3, and the rest of the row back onto itself. Press, starch, and trim.

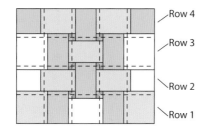

Fanned seam for Block A, Rows 1, 2, 3, and 4

7. Finally, sew on Row 5, and fan the middle white square back onto itself as for Row 1, pressing the rest of the seams on either side toward Row 4. Press, starch, and trim.

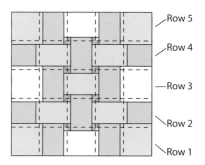

Fanned seams for Block A

8. Turn the block over and measure from raw edge to raw edge, from the pink square in Row 1 to the raw edge of the other pink square. (You will have to hold open the seam allowance to do this.) Did you come up with 3½"? If so, your seam allowance is great, and your fabric is working with you.

Do you remember what to do if it does not come out to 3½"? Remember YUM (page 85)? If your measurement is smaller or larger than 3½", you must make adjustments to the width you cut the middle strips for the 2 strip sets for Block B. For example, if you came up with 3⅝", this is YUM. Instead of trying to stretch out Block B to "make it fit," you are going to compensate in your cutting. The wide white strip for Rows 1 and 3 will be cut at YUM (3⅝") instead of 3½". The same goes for the wide white strip for Row 2.

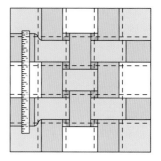

Measuring for YUM for Block B

Again, if your measurement came out right at 3½" (or 1 or 2 threads under or over), you are ready to make Block B.

Making Block B

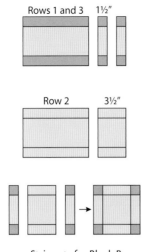

Strip sets for Block B

For Rows 1 and 3, you will need to cut 3 strips of pink 1½" wide, and 1½ strips of white 3½" wide (or YUM). For Row 2, you will need 3 strips of white cut 1½" wide, and 1½ strips of white cut 3½" wide (or YUM). You will need 1½ strip sets of each.

1. Sew the strip sets together as you did for Block A. For the Row 1 and 3 strip set, press the seams toward the pink. For Row 2, press the seams in toward the large square. Press, starch, and (if necessary) trim the strips.

2. Once the strip sets have been assembled, cut the Row 1 and 3 strip set into 34 segments 1½" wide. Cut the Row 2 strip set into 17 segments 3½" wide.

3. Make stacks of the rows and sew these together—Row 2 to Row 1. Press the seam toward Row 1, starch, and trim.

4. Sew Row 3 to Row 2, press toward Row 3, starch, and trim. That's it for block construction!

Assembling the quilt top

Lay out your quilt as shown below.

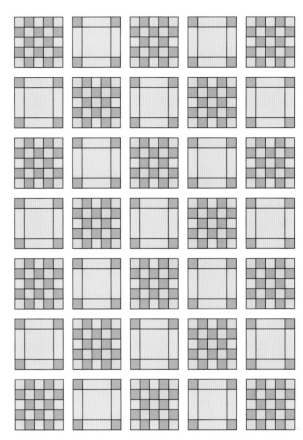

Double Irish Chain baby quilt layout

Because of the way you pressed the seams, no matter which way Block A is turned, its seams will butt up perfectly with Block B.

1. Once your quilt has been laid out, pick up the rows of blocks as you have done with other projects. You will have 7 stacks of 5 blocks each.

2. Set the stacks beside your machine, and sew Block 2 for all rows to Block 1, and so on. In each row, press the seams toward Block B, so that everything will butt up when you sew the rows together.

And that's it. You have yet another pretty little quilt made!

border information for this quilt
The first four small borders on this quilt all finish to 1" wide, and the outer border finishes at 5" wide. Refer to Class 180 for details.

PROJECT: HARRIET'S *IRISH CHAIN VARIATION* QUILT

This quilt introduces the idea of using a variety of fabrics. This gives it a more "scrappy" look than the other quilts in this book. It has two different blocks. Each of the A blocks is made up of two different fabrics plus the background. The B block consistently uses two colors—the chain color and the background. Feel free to make all the A blocks the same fabric combination if that is more to your taste.

Quilt top size: 37½" × 52½" (without borders)

Grid size: 1½"

Block size: 7½" × 7½"

Blocks:

18 Block A

17 Block B

Layout: 5 rows of 7 blocks each

Yardage for quilt top:

1 strip 2" wide of up to 36 different fabrics

½ yard blue fabric (chain fabric)

2 yards background fabric

CONSTRUCTING BLOCK A

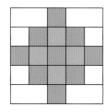

Block A

Irish Chain Variation

There are 2 different approaches to piecing Block A. If you are using only a limited number of colors and repeating them several times, it would be easiest to make the nine-patch that is in the center of each block, then build around it. You could make short strip sets and get several of the same color combination quickly. Because this quilt is so scrappy, it is more efficient to cut the pieces to size and piece them together in rows.

As in *Double Irish Chain*, there are 3 different rows, 2 of them repeated twice.

Rows 1 and 5

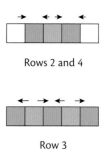

Rows 2 and 4

Row 3

You will be making 18 blocks, using different dark and light combinations for each. The background remains the same for all blocks.

Rows 1 & 5

For each block cut:

2 pieces 3½" × 4½" of the background fabric

1 piece 2" × 4½" of the dark print fabric

Stitch the first 2 strips together using the illustration below for color placement. Press the seam allowances toward the dark square, and measure the width to ensure the accuracy of the strips. Add the third strip, and repeat pressing and measuring. Cut 2 segments, each 2″ wide, from this strip set.

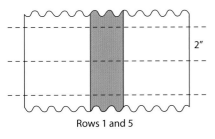

Rows 1 and 5

Cutting segments

Rows 2 & 4

For each block cut:

1 piece 2″ × 8½″ of the background fabric

1 piece 2″ × 8½″ of the dark print fabric

1 square 2″ × 2″ of the medium print fabric

Stitch the two 8½″ strips together. Press toward the dark strip. Cut 4 segments 2″ wide from the strip set. Join 2 of the segments by adding the 2″ square of medium print between them, the dark print next to the medium print, and the background at the ends. Press again toward the dark. Repeat for Row 4.

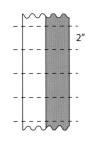

Rows 2 and 4

Join two strips, cut, and add single unit

Row 3

For each block cut:

1 piece 2″ × 4½″ of the dark print fabric

1 piece 2″ × 4½″ of the medium print fabric

Stitch these 2 strips together. Press the seam toward the dark print. Cut into 2 segments 2″ wide. Lay these segments end to end, and join. Add a 2″ square of dark print at one end of the segments.

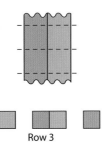

Row 3

Joining segments and square

Now you are ready to sew the 5 rows together. Lay them in order and sew 2 rows at time, pressing after each seam. When pressing Rows 1 and 2, as well as Rows 4 and 5, press the seam allowances toward Row 1 and Row 5. This will allow the 2 blocks to have seams that will butt together when you start to join the blocks into rows. Because this block is a checkerboard, and all the seams were pressed toward the fabric used most—the dark print—all the seams are ready to butt exactly.

Continue to make A blocks until you have 18.

Block B

Because there are only 2 fabrics used in all the B blocks, construction can be a bit different. You will see a nine-patch in the center of the block. You can make these units first from a long strip set, and then make strip sets to accommodate the top and bottom rows as well as the side units.

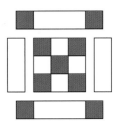

Breakout of rows

To make the 17 nine-patch units, you will need to cut:

Rows 1 & 3

2 strips 2″ × 42″ wide of chain fabric

1 strip 2″ × 42″ wide of background fabric

Sew 2 strip sets from the above strips. The background strip is between the chain fabric strips. Press the seams toward the chain fabric.

Cut 34 segments 2″ wide from this strip set.

Rows 1 and 3

Row 2

1 strip 2″ × 42″ wide of chain fabric

2 strips 2″ × 42″ wide of background fabric

Sew 2 strip sets from the above strips. The chain fabric is between the background strips. Press the seams toward the chain fabric.

Cut 17 segments 2″ wide from this strip set.

Row 2

Lay out the rows and construct the nine-patch units. You can fan the seams if you wish.

Next, you will add the strips of background to the sides of the nine-patch units.

Cut 34 pieces of background fabric 2″ × 5″. Stitch onto opposite sides of each nine-patch unit. Press the seams toward the background strips. Using a narrow ruler, check that the block is perfectly square so far, measuring from the seams.

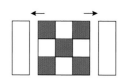

Add side strips.

The last part of this block is the Row 1 and 5 section. This will be another strip set.

Cut 2 strips 2″ × 42″ wide of chain fabric.

Cut 1 strip 5″ × 42″ wide of background fabric.

note Remember to measure from raw edge to raw edge of the nine-patch to make sure that the measurement is 5″. If it is not, cut the background to the exact same measurement as the nine-patch. We are determining YUMs again!

Sew the strips together, placing the background between the 2 chain fabric strips. Sew the first 2 strips, press toward the background fabric, and measure for width accuracy. Add the opposite chain fabric strip, press, and measure.

Rows 1 and 5

Cut 34 segments 2″ wide from this strip set.

Stitch these sections to opposite sides of the nine-patch unit.

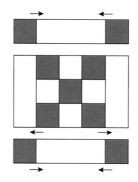

Add Rows 1 and 5 onto nine-patch unit.

On your design wall or a large open area on the floor, begin laying out the blocks as illustrated. Because the A blocks are scrappy, you might find that you don't care for some color combinations to sit next to one another. Moving the blocks around to create a pleasing appearance can be fun. Once the blocks are where you want them, pick up the rows in stacks, and proceed with constructing the rows and finally the quilt top.

We hope you have had fun working with a scrappy quilt for a change. There will be more to come in future books in this series.

Layout for quilt top

border information for this quilt
This quilt has a single wide border that finishes at 6″ wide.

Class 180

Adding borders to your quilt top is a wonderful way to frame the design developed by the piecing. The border is a place where you can stop the repeat piecing design and give your eye a place to stop or rest.

A single border is often enough for a simple quilt pattern. A combination of two or more plain strips around the outside edge of the piecing can be more exciting, and adding corner blocks can add another design element.

For now, we will keep the borders basic and simple. Further into the series, we will address more complex borders, such as pieced borders and border stripes. When you use a pattern as a guide for making a quilt, the cutting measurements are mathematically correct. However, as you now know from working through the patterns, mathematically correct measurements are very difficult to maintain when working with fabric, seam allowances, and pressing. This class will address how to work with the *actual* measurements of your quilt top. You can pick any quilt you have made up until now to use for these lessons.

LESSON ONE: Checking the quilt for squareness

Once the quilt top is completed and well pressed, you need to check that it is square. Are the two sides the same length, and are the top and bottom the same width? Then you'll need to measure the entire top to determine the length needed for the borders. The first step is to fold the quilt top in half to determine whether the top and bottom are the same width as the center, and the two sides are the same length. To do this, fold one end of the top over to the center of the quilt top as shown at right. Are the top and center the same width? Repeat with the other end.

Do the same with the sides, one side at a time. Are they the same length?

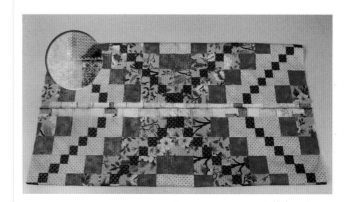

Folding quilt top to center

> *tip* When measuring for borders, do not measure along the actual outside edge, since it's easy to stretch that edge as you measure.

HOW TO CORRECT FOR DEVIATIONS

As you pieced your quilt top, you squared up each unit as you went along. This process really helps develop a quilt top that is very accurate. If everything is perfectly even, you're ready to measure and cut the border strips. But what if things don't come out even? Perhaps one side is longer than the other, or one end is shorter than the other. Now is the time to make corrections.

Harriet does this by examining the piecing of the seams where the rows are joined. It is a common problem for the fabric to pivot slightly as you're nearing the end of any seam, especially if you are using a zigzag throat plate. If this is happening, then it's possible that a slightly larger or smaller seam was taken at the edge, making that side of the quilt shorter (or longer) or narrower (or wider) than the opposite side where the seam started. Just one or two threads' width difference per seam can throw off the measurements dramatically. If this is the case, restitch, being careful to keep the needle just beside the previous stitching. If the seams need to be smaller, release the stitches back from the edge about 3″ to 4″, and restitch, being careful to not stitch in the same holes a second time.

> **hint** When folding your quilt top in half, line up the seams of corresponding blocks. This often shows which seams or blocks are off. They should line up exactly across from one another.

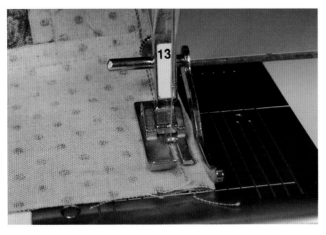

A deeper seam being taken

Whatever you determine, attempt to make corrections until the top is within ⅛″ or less of being even when it is folded in half and measured.

Check for accuracy by folding the edge to the center after each correction. You don't want to overcorrect. Often one correction is enough to fix the problem. In the end, you want both sides to be exactly the same length, and both the top and bottom to be the same width. *Never cut or trim to correct size discrepancies!*

LESSON TWO: Using a ruler to straighten edges

Next, use a square ruler 16″ or larger to check all four corners. Are they perfectly square, at perfect 90° angles? When placing a square ruler on the corner, use the straight and diagonal lines of the ruler to align with the inner seams of the blocks.

Everything needs to be aligned with the ruler lines as closely and as parallel as possible. If the corner is not perfectly square, shave away any little bits that are causing the problem. *Remember—do not do this before you check the length and width of each side of the quilt top. You cannot correct an internal piecing problem by whacking off the corner to make the sides and the top and bottom the correct length. This action will only distort the shape and measurements of the units in the corner.*

If the corner is really out of square, look at the internal piecing of the block in the corner. Adjust the seam allowances first as described, and if the corner is not perfectly square, you can then shave off threads to correct this.

This is very important because when the first border is sewn on, the border will continue the out-of-square problem, and the finished quilt will not lie flat or hang straight.

Use a 24″-long ruler and rotary cutter to clean up the side edges of the quilt top. Measure out from any seams to make sure that you are not cutting too deep into the body of the quilt top. Remember, you are just cleaning up the edge of ragged threads. The edge pieces should measure the grid measurement plus ¼″. If you cut too deeply, the dimensions of the units within the block along the edge will not stay accurate. For example, if the squares of your four-patch should finish at 2″, but you cut into the side of one or more of these squares, they will not measure 2″ finished and will not appear square when the quilt is finished.

Once the top and bottom of the quilt top are even with the center (the same length as the center on both sides), and the corners are square, you're ready to measure for and cut your borders.

A SLICK TRICK FOR ACCURATE BORDER WIDTH

In the next lesson, you'll learn about border length. But width must be addressed, too. Harriet strongly recommends that each border strip be cut *at least 1" wider than the desired finished measurement.*

You will find that when you stitch the border onto a pieced quilt top, going over the lumpy seam allowances and not sewing every seam 100% straight will affect the width of the border after it is pressed. If you've added extra width, the border can now be cut perfectly straight using the seam as a baseline.

For example, if the border is designed to finish at 4", lay the ruler on the seam at the 4¼" line, and cut along the raw edge of the border. This will give you an exact-width border and a very straight edge to add the next border (if any) onto. Do this for every border you add.

If this is the last border, do not trim it until the quilting is finished. This extra gives you a handle to hold onto when quilting right up to the seamline.

LESSON THREE:
Measuring for border lengths

Measure through the center of your quilt top, end to end, to determine the length of the side borders. If you choose to add the top and bottom borders first, measure through the center from side to side.

> *tip* There are no solid rules about which borders go on first—whether it's sides, then top and bottom, or top and bottom, then sides. It depends on what appeals to you. Look at the illustrations below and notice your first reaction to each. If you feel one is balanced and the other is not, you'll probably prefer to attach your borders in that order, or vice versa. We do recommend, however, that you be consistent when you're adding several plain strip borders to the same quilt.

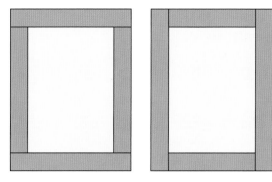

Different effects of border placement

The side border length is determined by the measurement through the center of the quilt, from top to bottom.

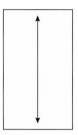

Measure through center of quilt.

The top and bottom borders are cut the width of the top through the center, plus the width of the two side borders. It is best to attach the side borders first, and then measure the width from the raw edge of one border through the center to the raw edge of the opposite border.

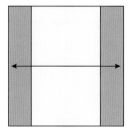

Measure from raw edge to raw edge of borders.

> *tip* Harriet likes to cut her border strips about 1" longer than measured. This gives a bit of overhang to trim and square once each border is attached. It is critical that every corner is perfectly square before adding the next border. By having a bit of extra length added, there is actually something to trim and square up. Be sure to mark in ½" for the starting point of the border on the edge of the quilt.

CUTTING EXTRA-WIDE FOR ACCURACY

Many quilters prefer to cut border pieces from the length of the fabric, using a continuous piece for each side. Others cut crosswise strips (selvage to selvage) and piece the strips to get the length needed. (Sometimes your choice is dictated by the design of the fabric; for example, you would usually cut stripes lengthwise.)

If you cut crosswise, you must add together measurements for the top, bottom, and two sides. You will also need to add four times the width of the border to this total to allow for the extra length added to the top and bottom borders by the width of the side borders. Remember to add ½″ or more to the strip width for trimming, plus ½″ seam allowances.

Let's walk through this step by step. You are adding a 4″ border to a baby quilt. The quilt top measures 25½″ × 35½″. You need 2 strips the length of the quilt, or 35½″ of border for each side (the ½″ is seam allowance). That equals 71″ of fabric.

The top and bottom borders are sewn on after the side borders, so their length will be 25½″ plus the width of the side borders. If you are adding 4″ borders, that would be an additional 8″ plus ½″ seam allowance—a total of 33½″. Total inches needed would be 35.5″ + 35.5″ + 33.5″ + 33.5″ = 138″.

If you are cutting borders from the length of the fabric, you would need to buy enough to accommodate the longest border (35½″, or 1 yard). If the borders are cut 4½″ wide, you will be using 18″ of the width of the yardage, leaving 1 yard of 24″-wide fabric. This 24″ is now available for strips when making the blocks. When figuring yardage for the blocks, figure 24″ strips instead of 42″, and you will be able to use this excess fabric and know how much more you need to cut as 42″ strips. No leftovers.

If you are cutting the borders crosswise and piecing the strips together, divide the total number of inches you need by the fabric width. So, 138″ ÷ 42″ = 3.29, or 4 strips. Four strips 4½″ wide = 18″ (½ yard) of fabric.

The basic formula for borders with *butted* corners is as follows:

First border length = finished border length + 1″. (Remember to add the width of the border × 2 for the top and bottom to accommodate the width of the side borders once they are attached.)

If a quilt will have multiple borders, this formula continues. To minimize confusion, draw a diagram and write your numbers on it.

ADDING MULTIPLE BORDERS

What if, instead of adding one wide border, you want to add two narrow borders plus a wide one? Using the diagram below, let's walk through the measurements.

Your quilt top finished at 25½″ × 35½″. We want to add 2 borders 1″ wide and finish with a 4″ border. How do we know what size border strips to cut? The first side borders will be the length of the quilt top—35½″ (seam allowance included). Once they are sewn on, measure from raw edge to raw edge of the borders. With the seam allowance added, that is an additional 2½″, plus the 25″ of the quilt top. The first top and bottom borders will be 27½″. The new length of the quilt is: 35″ + 2½″ = 37½″ long.

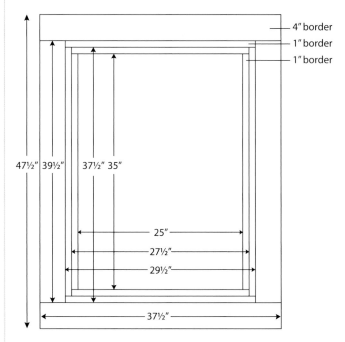

Diagram showing border sizes

You have added the first 1″ border to all sides of your quilt top. The quilt is now 27½″ × 37½″, and you want to add another 1″ border to the first 1″ border. The side measurement is 37½″, so you will need 2 strips 37½″ long. The top and bottom borders will need to be 27½" + the 1" width × 2 = 27½" + 2" = 29½".

If the border is cut lengthwise, you will need to buy 1 yard of the second border. If the border is cut crosswise, add the lengths together: 37.5" + 37.5" + 29.5" + 29.5" = 134". Divide the number of inches needed by the fabric width: 134" ÷ 42" = 3.19, or 4 strips. Four strips 1.5" wide = 6" (¼ yard).

Keep repeating this process as you work through the wide third border in the diagram. The drawing makes it easy to keep the measurements straight.

Second border length = finished border length + (finished border width × 2) + 1".

Continue this process with every border that you want to add.

PIECING BORDERS

If the borders will be longer than the available strip length, you'll need to piece them. The angle of the seam is a personal preference, but we feel that a 45° angle is the least noticeable. Again, some fabrics will look best with the seam angled, while some may not show a straight seam at all. This will be for you to decide with each situation and fabric. If the fabric is a busy print, chances are the seams will never show either way. However, if it's a solid fabric, the seam can be obvious. Study the illustration below to get a feel for what your eye prefers.

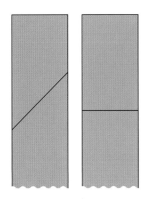

How to splice a border seam

For a diagonal border seam, lay the strips on top of one another, all facing right side up. Using the 45° angle on your long ruler, cut through all the layers. That way, when you position 2 strips right sides together, the angle is correct for both ends. Align the edges and make sure that the offset on either end is no more than your seam allowance width.

When you start to stitch, the needle should align perfectly with the "crotch" made by the 2 angles coming together. The edge of the fabric should align exactly with your seam allowance guide. Stitch, and press the seam open. If the border edges are not exactly straight, the seam was not aligned correctly.

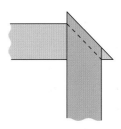

Placement of seam for diagonal joining

PINNING FOR A PERFECT FIT

You've measured your quilt. You've cut and, where necessary, seamed strips together to create the border length needed. Now you're ready to attach those strips to the body of the quilt.

Here is one of our firm rules in quiltmaking: *Always cut borders to size and pin them to the quilt top prior to sewing.*

Never merely take the strips and the quilt top to the sewing machine and start feeding them through the machine. You must always carefully pin the strips to the edges of the quilt top before sewing.

1. Make placement marks on the strips before pinning. Fold each border in half lengthwise to find its center, and mark with a pin. Place a pin at the end edge measurements if you're cutting the border a bit longer than the actual measurement of the quilt top. Find the midway point between the center and end edges and place a pin at this position on both sides of the center. Repeat this process on the quilt top.

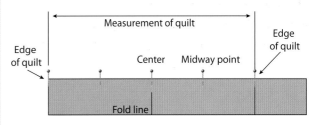

Measuring and marking center points

2. When pinning the borders to the quilt top, we recommend that you work at the ironing board or on a large table. You will be adding 1 border at a time. Lay your quilt top face up. Start at the center. Match the center pin on the border to the center pin on the quilt top. Pin the border in place. Place the heads of the pins alongside the raw edges, making it easier to remove them as you come to them when sewing. Line up the other placement pins on the border with the placement pins of the quilt top.

3. Pin the border securely to the top between these marker pins. Take care to pin the seam allowances down so they can't flip as you stitch the border onto the edge.

4. Take the top to the sewing machine and sew with the border on top, taking out the pins as you go.

> *tip* If you find that either the border or the quilt top is slightly longer than the area between the pins, ease the fullness in evenly, and pin carefully. When you sew, place the longer side down. Allow the feed dogs to help ease in the fullness. If the longer piece is on top, you are more likely to get small pleats at the pins.

5. Back at the ironing board, press the seam in the closed position. Fold the border over and glide the iron from the quilt top across the seam allowance, gently pushing the seam allowance toward the border strip. Once the seam is set, apply starch to make sure the border seam is crisp and flat.

6. Repeat Steps 2 through 5 for the opposite side, and for the top and bottom borders. Once all 4 borders have been attached, pressed, and starched, you are ready to trim and square.

7. If you have cut the borders wider than needed (see page 96), now is the time to trim them to size. Measure each corner with the square ruler again and check for squareness. Make any corrections that are necessary before adding the next round of strips. Keeping the borders flat and accurate is easy if you make them wider and you square and trim each time a round of borders is added.

LESSON FOUR:
Borders with mitered corners

It is truly a personal choice as to whether mitered or butted corners are best on a quilt, unless you're using a stripe or other directional print. Stripes really frame the quilt nicely when mitered. Mitered corners do take more fabric and more time, but the results can be well worth the effort. In this book, we will deal only with adding a single mitered border; in later books in the series, we will talk about adding multiple borders and mitering them.

1. The first step in mitering is to measure the length of the quilt top. To that measurement, add 2 times the width of the border, plus 5″. This is the length you need to cut or piece the side border.

> For example, if the quilt top is 60″ square and the borders are 6″ wide, you'll need border strips that are 77″ long (60″ + 12″ + 5″ = 77″). Cut or piece 2 border strips this length.

2. Pin securely, and stitch the strips to the sides of the quilt top. Do not stitch off the edge of the quilt top. Stop and backstitch at the seam allowance line, ¼″ in from the raw edge. The excess length will extend beyond each edge. Press the seams toward the border.

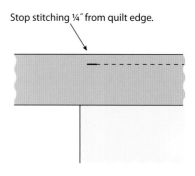
Stop stitching ¼″ from quilt edge.

3. Determine the length needed for the top and bottom border in the same way, measuring through the center of the quilt to the raw edges of each border. Add 5″ to this measurement. Cut or piece these border strips.

4. Again, pin and stitch up to the seamline, and backstitch. Each side of each corner is stitched just up to the seamline and not beyond. The border strips extend beyond each end. Once the borders are on, press the seams toward the borders.

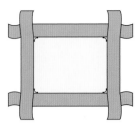

Excess border length extends beyond each end.

5. To create the miter, position a corner on the ironing board, supporting the quilt top so that it doesn't drag and distort the corner. Working with the quilt right side up, lay the unstitched end of one border out straight and flat and then lay the other border out crossing the first border.

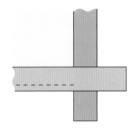

Position border strips for mitering.

6. Fold the top border strip under so that it meets the edge of the bottom border and forms a 45° angle. If the border is a plaid or stripe, make sure that the patterns match along the folded edge. Press the fold in place.

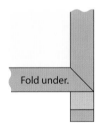

Fold under top border strip 45°.

7. Pin the fold in place. Position a 90°-angle ruler over the corner to check that the corner is flat and square. When everything is in place, remove the pins, and press the fold firmly.

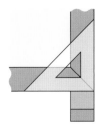

Checking for square corner

8. Using a water-soluble gluestick or even Elmer's Washable School Glue (make sure it is the totally water-soluble variety), draw a fine line of glue just under the fold of the miter. Press to set the glue. Now you can fold the quilt top so that the right sides are together. The glue will hold the fold in place perfectly while you sew.

Gluing corner in place

9. Beginning at the inside corner, backstitch, and stitch on the fold toward the outside point, being careful not to allow any stretching to occur.

Stitching on fold line—wrong side of quilt

10. Once the seam has been stitched, open to the right side and check that everything is aligned properly. If it is, gently tug on the glued area; it will release easily. Trim the excess border fabric to a ¼″ seam allowance. Press the seam open. Repeat for the other 3 corners.

note As discussed earlier, Harriet suggests that the final border be cut wider than the desired finished width so that there is a margin for control while quilting, as well as the ability to cut a perfectly straight and even final border after quilting. When figuring yardage for the borders, don't forget to add 1″ to 2″ to the width of the final border to accommodate this situation.

Class 190

QUILTING

We really want to emphasize that *you are not a quilter until you quilt your own quilt tops!* One of the most satisfying experiences in quiltmaking is when the quilting is done, the binding is on, and the quilt is washed, allowing all the texture to come up from the batting. When you lay it on a bed, hang it on a wall, or spread it on a table, the excitement comes from the quilting just as much as from the fabrics you have used.

It is our sincere hope that you will not join the thousands of "toppers" in the quilt world and neatly fold up the new tops you have created, lay them on a closet shelf, and start making even more. There will come a time when you go back to the stack and find that you don't even like the ones on the bottom anymore.

We also hope that you will take the time to learn to do your own quilting. There is always the lure of the instant gratification you get from sending your quilt tops to a professional quilter. You can continue to sew, and someone else does the quilting for you. This might seem easy at first, but there will come a day when you make a really awesome quilt top and you want it to be yours in every way—from the fabric selection to the binding. That is not the time to start learning how to quilt! If you start learning the very simple basic techniques of machine quilting as you are learning to piece, you will be amazed at how easy it is, and how rewarding it can be to tell everyone, "I made it myself!" Finish the tops as you go and enjoy them! Isn't the look and feel of a real quilt the reason you started this in the first place?

note As we have stated before, we do not teach the actual quilting in this book. In our opinion, the best workbook for learning how to machine quilt is Harriet's book Heirloom Machine Quilting (see Resources, page 112). It has been in continuous publication for over 22 years and is in its fourth revised edition. It is the most thorough and up-to-date book on learning to quilt you can use, so we send you there for the actual quilting instructions.

This class will cover backings and bindings, which aren't addressed in *Heirloom Machine Quilting*. At the end of the class, you will find quilting design ideas in Lesson Four.

LESSON ONE: Quilt backing

When choosing a backing (also known as a lining) for your quilt, think about letting it complement the front. It used to be that most backings were solids or muslin, but many backings are now made from prints or even pieced units.

If you're an excellent quilter, a solid fabric will really show off your quilting. However, if you're new to quilting, a print will camouflage any uneven stitches or contrasting threads.

The backing fabric must be the same fiber content, quality of cloth, weight, and thread count as the fabrics used for the top. Although a limited number of prints, as well as muslin, are available in 90″ widths or wider for backings, the majority of fabrics used for backings are 45″ wide.

DETERMINING YARDAGE

To determine the yardage needed for backing, be sure to add 2″ to 3″ to the size of the quilt top on all four sides. It helps to make a sketch of the quilt top measurements in order to determine what seams might be needed, and whether to make them horizontal or vertical for the best use of the yardage. The illustration below shows various seam configurations to use in calculations. When figuring yardage, don't forget to subtract the width of the selvages, as they need to be removed before you piece the lengths together. The standard width used to figure yardage is 42″.

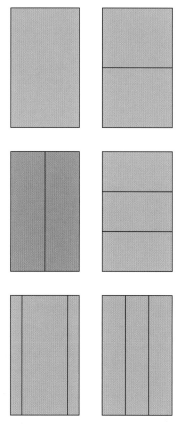

Backing seam placement options

Following are backing yardage guidelines for various quilt sizes.

Quilt tops 40″ wide or *narrower* require only 1 length of fabric (plus 4″ to 5″) because the fabric is wide enough to accommodate the width of the quilt top.

Quilt tops 40″ wide or *wider* require 2 pieces of fabric seamed together. If you buy 2 lengths of fabric to back a quilt 60″ long, you need 3½ yards ([64″ × 2] ÷ 36″ = 3.56, or 3½ yards). If the quilt is 44″ wide, and the seams will run horizontally, you would need only 2⅔ yards ([48″ × 2] ÷ 36″ = 2.67 = 2⅔ yards). Quite a savings!

Horizontal seams utilize the width of the fabric with the least left over.

Twin and throw-sized quilts are generally around 72″ wide or square. Using the yardage formula below, we find that 2 widths of fabric are needed. If the quilt is 72″ × 90″ and the seams are vertical, you need 5¼ yards. Horizontal seams would require 3 widths, requiring 6 yards. Therefore, vertical seams would be the best choice.

Full-sized quilts average 81″ × 96″ finished. Again, 2 widths will just be wide enough, requiring 5⅓ yards. Horizontal seams would require 8 yards.

Queen-sized quilts average 90″ × 108″ finished. Three widths of fabric (about 9½ yards) are required for vertical seams, but only 8 yards for horizontal seams. Note: If you choose to use vertical seams, they appear the most balanced if you keep 1 full width in the center. Divide the remaining width equally between the remaining 2 lengths, and sew them on either side of the center panel.

King-sized quilts are generally 120″ × 120″. A full 3 widths, each 3½ yards long—a total of 10½ yards—are needed for the backing, regardless of which direction the seams run, as the quilt is square.

These yardages are just examples based on the specific quilt sizes given. It is easy to figure backing yardage if you simply plug your quilt top sizes into the yardage formula.

> *tip* *yardage formula*
>
> An easy formula for yardage calculation is as follows:
>
> Quilt top width ÷ fabric width (minus selvages) = number of lengths of backing needed (round up to the nearest whole number)
>
> Then:
>
> Quilt top length (in inches) × number of lengths needed ÷ 36″ = number of yards to buy

We recommended that you lightly starch your unwashed backing fabric before using it. If you prewash the fabric, starching it is *strongly* recommended.

Refer to *Heirloom Machine Quilting* (see Resources, page 112) for complete instructions on layering, pin basting, and quilting your quilt.

LESSON TWO: Preparing the quilt for binding

Once the layers have been quilted, you are ready to prepare the edges for binding. You will need to first remove the excess batting and backing from the edges, square the corners, and straighten the edges.

There are two schools of thought about preparing to bind a quilt. Some quilters leave the batting and backing in place until the binding has been attached, then trim the excess away. We prefer the more traditional method of trimming the edges of all three layers, then applying the binding. Try both, and choose which you prefer and get the best results from.

SQUARING UP THE QUILT TOP

1. To trim the edges, use a long, wide ruler and a large square ruler. Starting in a corner, use the square ruler to check for squareness, and trim the edges. Be sure that you align the ruler lines with the seamlines within the body of the quilt.

note This photo shows trimming off extra width added to final border size as discussed on page 97 (Cutting extra-wide for accuracy).

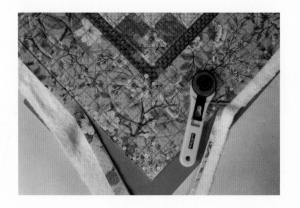

Aligning ruler lines with seamlines in quilt

2. Trim the sides, keeping the border width accurate and aligning with the corner cuts. Repeat this for all 4 sides.

3. Fold the quilt ends in to the center to make sure that all the widths are the same. Repeat for the sides.

4. If the quilting runs right up to the raw edge, you won't have to add additional stabilization. If the edges are loose, we suggest that you machine baste the edges together (using long stitches) to eliminate the possibility of distortion when

sewing on the binding. Note: When basting by machine, be very careful not to stretch the edges as they pass under the foot. A walking foot is a great help in this process.

LESSON THREE: Basic binding

The quilt top has been pieced, layered, and quilted. All that now remains is to close up the edges, and, at long last, your quilt will be finished, ready to wash and use. It is an exciting step ahead, and one you must not rush through. It's important that the binding looks as nice as the rest of the quilt. If the binding is sloppy and poorly attached and finished, it detracts from the whole quilt. Your finish work is critical to the look of the finished product.

STRAIGHT-GRAIN DOUBLE-FOLD BINDING

There are several different options for preparing binding, but for now, we will address the easiest—straight-grain double-fold binding.

note It is a common belief that bias binding makes a stronger edge for a quilt and will last longer, especially on a bed quilt, because the wear and tear is spread over a diagonal web of threads rather than being positioned along only one or two threads as it is in straight-grain binding. However, bias grain on a straight-edge quilt is stretchy, and, if care is not taken, it can stretch when applied and cause rippling along the edge. The choice between straight-grain and bias binding will be based on personal preference as you gain experience with both later in your quilting adventure. For now, let's stay with the easiest binding. The quilt tops that you have made throughout this course have straight edges, so there is no real need for bias.

Harriet is a bit unorthodox when it comes to binding grainline. She uses neither straight grain nor true bias, but a bit of both. When fabric is taken from the bolt, it's generally not on grain without some straightening. Instead of straightening the grain, Harriet cuts her strips from the off-grain fabric. This provides strips that are not perfectly on grain yet not true bias. This gives her the best of both methods, since the grain is slightly off, allowing more threads to take the wear, but the strips not nearly as stretchy as bias binding.

Double-fold binding is made from strips cut from 1¼" to 2¼" wide and folded in half. This is also known as French Fold binding. The width of the strip depends on the thickness of the batting used and how wide you want the finished binding to be. If you're reproducing a quilt from the 1800s, you'll want your binding to be as narrow as you can possibly work with—generally ¼" wide or narrower, finished—for authenticity. These strips would be cut 1¼" to 1½" wide and sewn on with a ⅛" seam allowance.

A really nice-looking binding for most quilts is about ⅜" finished, using 2" cut strips doubled and a scant ¼" seam allowance. Regardless of the width of binding you choose, remember that once it's wrapped around the edge of the quilt, it should not be empty, but filled completely with the batting and quilt layers.

CUTTING BINDING STRIPS

Cut binding strips 4 times the desired finished width plus ½" (or seam allowance needed per the chart below) for seam allowances AND ⅛" to ¼" to go around the thickness of the batting. The fatter the batting, the more you need to add here.

³⁄₁₆" binding = 1¼" cut	⅛" seam allowance
¼" binding = 1½" cut	³⁄₁₆" seam allowance
⁵⁄₁₆" binding = 1¾" cut	scant ¼" seam allowance
⅜" binding = 2" cut	¼" seam allowance
½" binding = 2¼" cut	generous ¼" seam allowance

To determine how much binding you need, calculate the perimeter (distance around your quilt). Figure 2 × the length + 2 × the width = the total inches of binding needed. For example, a quilt 60" × 80" would require 280" of binding.

We recommend that you add a minimum of 12" to this sum to allow for turning corners, piecing strips together, and joining the ends together on the quilt. So how many strips is this? If you do the figuring based on 42" strips (selvage to selvage), then 292" ÷ 42" = 6.95 strips needed. Round up to 7 strips across the width of the fabric times the cut width of the strip. This is how much yardage is needed.

The chart below gives you an estimate of the yardage needed to bind various sizes of quilts with straight-grain binding. These measurements are based on a ½" finished binding.

Estimated yardage for ½"-wide straight grain binding

Quilt Size	# of 2¼"-wide strips	Inches of fabric	Yards of fabric
Wallhanging (36" × 36")	4	9	¼
Twin (54" × 90")	7	16	½
Double (72" × 90")	8	18	½
Queen (90" × 108")	10	22½	⅝
King (120" × 120")	12	27	¾

✳ EXERCISE: BINDING THE EDGES OF YOUR QUILT

Binding is a several-step process: you join the cut strips together, stitch the binding to the quilt front, and then finish by stitching it to the back.

JOINING THE STRIPS TOGETHER

The strips need to be joined with a 45°-angle seam.

1. Keeping the strips double (wrong side to wrong side), position the 45° angle of the ruler on the edge of the strip as shown, then cut. Repeat with the remainder of the strips.

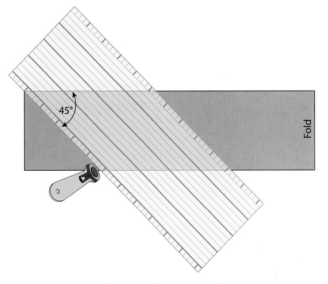

Position 45° angle of ruler, and cut.

2. To join the strips together, line up the edges, offsetting by ¼", and sew with a ¼" seam allowance.

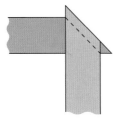

Join strip ends together.

3. Continue joining all the strips together into a continuous length. Press the seams open.

JOINING THE ENDS OF THE BINDING

There are several ways to finish the ends when attaching binding. Here is the easiest.

1. Cut and join the strips as explained above. Starch the strips, and press them in half lengthwise, wrong sides together. At one end of the strip, fold a ¼" seam allowance over to the wrong side, and press. The point from the wrong side of the binding should be on the bottom, as shown in the illustration.

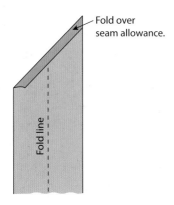

Fold ¼" seam allowance on 45° angle.

2. With the long fold open, position the binding on top of the quilt top. Start stitching the binding at the point, stitching through only 1 thickness of the binding. Stitch for about 4 inches.

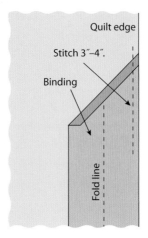

Stitch through one thickness from point.

3. Lift the presser foot and cut the threads. Fold the binding over to double. Start stitching about 1" below the short edge of the point. Stitch the binding in place, aligning the edges exactly and stopping ¼" from the corner.

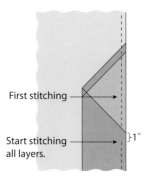

Fold binding over to double.

Stitch up to ¼"
(or your chosen seam allowance) from corner.

4. Turn the quilt so that you're lined up to sew the next side. Backstitch off edge. Fold the binding straight up toward the side you just sewed. Then refold toward the new edge, lining up the second fold with the outer edge of the quilt, and the raw edges of the binding with the raw edges of the quilt.

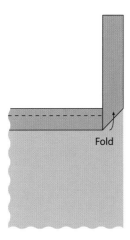

First fold for miter

5. Begin sewing at the outer edge of the quilt; sew through all the layers at the corner. Continue down the edge, repeating the corner treatment.

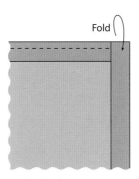

Second fold alignment

6. Once you've arrived back at the beginning, tuck the end of the binding into the pocket. Lower the needle into the fabric. Lay the end of the binding strip over the point and single thickness that was the starting point. Cut off the end just before the

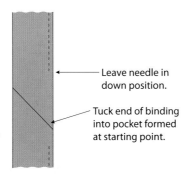

Leave needle in down position.

Tuck end of binding into pocket formed at starting point.

Tuck in end, and close stitching.

stitching that started going through all the layers. Tuck the end into the pocket, and finish closing the seam.

FINAL SEWING

If you blindstitch the binding by hand, we suggest that you use a 40-weight 3-ply hand quilting thread.

1. Wrap the binding around to the back of the quilt, placing the folded edge of the binding on top of the stitching line. You can either pin the binding in place, use binding clips to hold it, or glue it in place with Elmer's Washable School Glue. If using glue, apply a very small line, and press dry with the iron before hand stitching.

2. Begin the blind stitch by inserting the needle under the edge of the binding right at the fold edge of the binding. Next, put the needle into the quilt immediately across from where it is in the binding. You don't want to stitch through to the front—just into the batting. Let the needle travel approximately ¼″ through the inside of the quilt before emerging and traveling into the binding, again right at the edge. Continue in this manner.

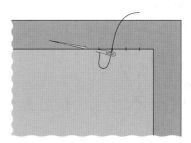

Finish edge with blind stitching.

3. When you reach the corners, you'll find that the corner (miter) is already formed on the top of the quilt, but you'll need to coax the miter on the back with your fingers. Fold 1 side down, then the other, creating a neat miter. The fold should be opposite that on the front side, with the bulk evenly distributed on both sides. This creates a flat corner.

Quilting design ideas

You will find that choosing quilting designs is as difficult as choosing fabric, if not more so! It seems that most books and patterns totally ignore this very important step and leave it up to the reader with the dreaded phrase "quilt as desired."

As a new quilter, you probably don't yet know how you want to do the quilting. We have added some suggested ways to quilt the tops that you have made from this book. The quilting is very simple and is done mostly in straight lines, using a special walking foot. This is the easiest method to learn, and it can provide a great deal of texture without your having to learn free-motion quilting at this point.

We truly want you to learn to quilt as you progress through this series of books, so we will start simply. As the quilts become more complicated and the designs more complex, the quilting will do the same. This gives you a chance to make the tops to learn on as you go.

The following pages feature line drawings showing the actual quilting lines on the quilts in this book. These are suggested designs to get you started, but don't hesitate to use your creativity and do your own thing.

Happy quilting!

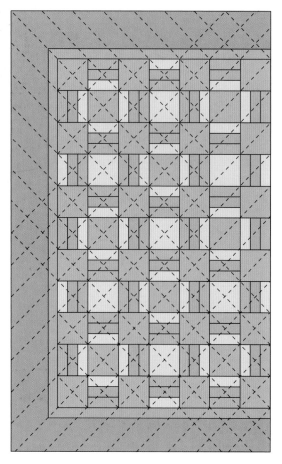

Woodland Winter

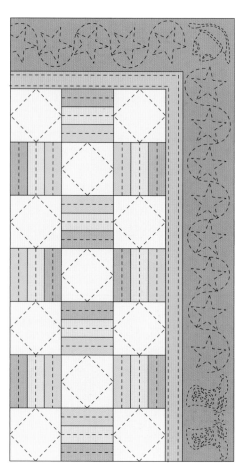

Cowboy Corral

Triple Rail Fence

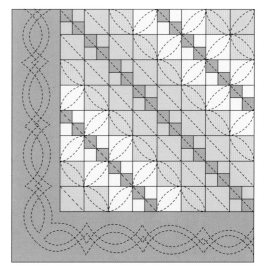

Town Square

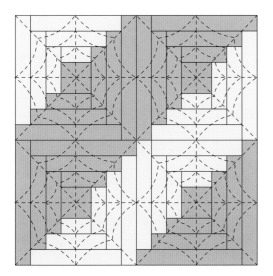

Patriotic Log Cabin

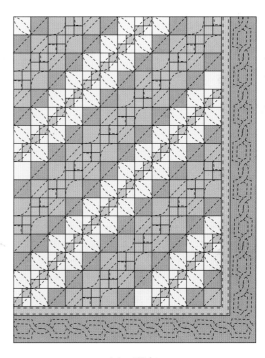

Asian Nights

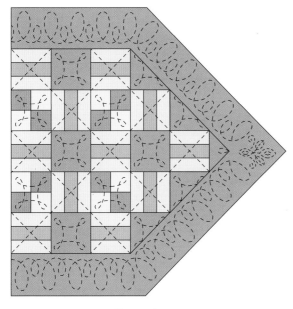

Country Lane

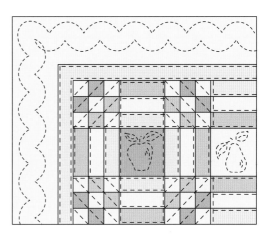

Interlacing Circles

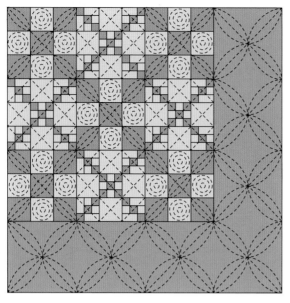

Double Nine-Patch Chain

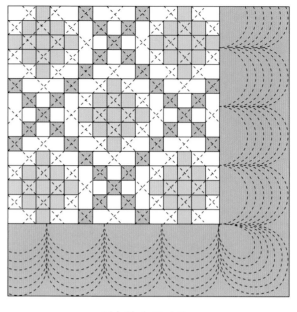

Irish Chain Variation

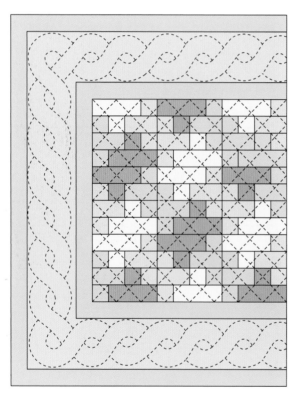

Inlaid Tile table runner

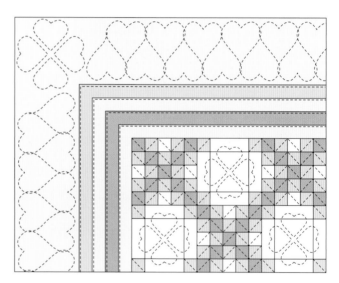

Double Irish Chain

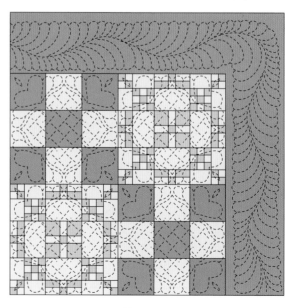

Homespun

Your Final

Now that you have worked through all the lessons and completed all the exercises, you are probably quite comfortable with basic squares and strips. Hopefully, you now understand how to break apart a pattern and find the units that make up the design. You can assign a size to the grid and figure out strip sets, and you can calculate yardage and generate a recipe for quilts that are made from just strips and squares. If you can do this, the book has achieved its purpose.

Below you will find a quilt that we have chosen as a final exam for this course. This quilt is based on a very old favorite, Burgoyne Surrounded, but we have simplified it by using only five pieced blocks, set together with large Nine-Patch blocks.

We have purposely not given any instructions for this quilt. We have provided a worksheet so that you can do your own calculations, choose your own grid, figure the yardage needed, and make a strip set recipe for yourself. The units are broken out to get you started. We hope that you will make this quilt to check your numbers and see how easy it is to plan quilts on your own.

Good luck!

Homespun

HOMESPUN WORKSHEET

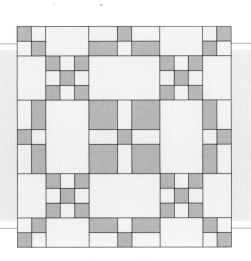

Homespun block

Units needed:

There are 6 different units needed to make this block; 4 are constructed using strips, and 2 are background fabric. Once you identify the units, count how many are in the block. Break the units into strip sets, and then figure how many inches of strip sets it will take to accommodate the units for all 5 blocks.

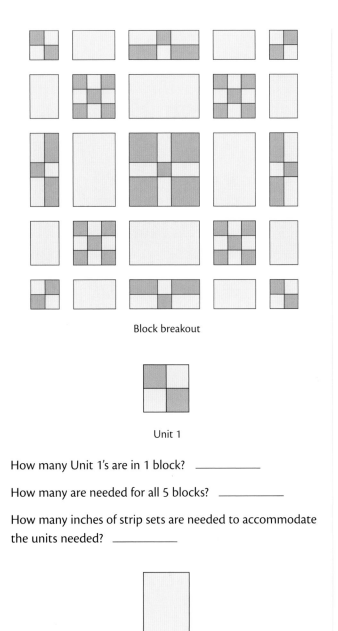

Block breakout

Unit 1

How many Unit 1's are in 1 block? _____

How many are needed for all 5 blocks? _____

How many inches of strip sets are needed to accommodate the units needed? _____

Unit 2

How many Unit 2's are in 1 block? _____

How many are needed for all 5 blocks? _____

How many inches of strip sets are needed to accommodate the units needed? _____

Unit 3

How many Unit 3's are in 1 block? _____

How many are needed for all 5 blocks? _____

How many inches of strip sets are needed to accommodate the units needed? _____

Unit 4

How many Unit 4's are in 1 block? _____

How many are needed for all 5 blocks? _____

How many inches of strip sets are needed to accommodate the units needed? _____

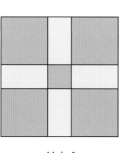

Unit 5

How many Unit 5's are in 1 block? _____

How many are needed for all 5 blocks? _____

How many inches of strip sets are needed to accommodate the units needed? _____

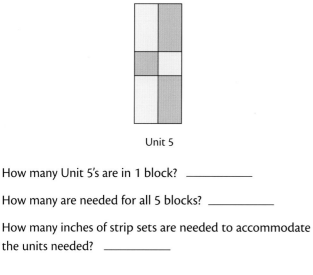

Unit 6

How many Unit 6's are in 1 block? _____

How many are needed for all 5 blocks? _____

How many inches of strip sets are needed to accommodate the units needed? _____

Referring to Class 170, Lessons One and Two, work the formula to determine how many strip sets are needed and how much yardage it will take to make the Burgoyne block.

Repeat the process for the large Nine-Patch block used as a connector block.

When you have completed the recipe, you are ready to put into practice everything you have learned up to this point, without guidance.

CONGRATULATIONS!

Once you have made this quilt, along with the rest of the quilts in the book, you are well on your way to becoming a master quilter!

We hope you have enjoyed this adventure into the beginnings of patchwork. You should be very proud of your work. If you followed all the instructions and worked carefully, we hope you will see that speed comes along with precision!

We look forward to continuing your education in the next book—Volume 2, which is all about strips and squares but with the added excitement of working with diagonal sets, incorporated borders, and sashings, plus more about borders and quilting and more wonderful quilts! By the time you finish this course, you should be ready to go.

Happy quilting!

Harriet & Carrie

About the authors

Harriet started quilting seriously in 1974, working alongside her mom. Her early quilting career included producing baby quilts for craft shows and teaching adult education classes. In 1981, Harriet opened her quilt shop, Harriet's Treadle Arts. Her specialties at the time were free-motion embroidery, machine arts, and machine quilting.

In 1982, Harriet attended one of Mary Ellen Hopkins's seminars. Mary Ellen's streamlined techniques and innovative design ideas led Harriet to a new way of thinking, which caused her to give up the machine arts and to teach only quilting. Today, she is world renowned for being a true "mover and shaker" in the quilt world. In the late 1990s, she was voted one of the "88 Leaders of the Quilt World."

Harriet created and inspired a whole new generation of machine quilters with her bestselling book *Heirloom Machine Quilting*, which has enjoyed 22 continuous years in print. She is also the author of *Mastering Machine Appliqué* and *From Fiber to Fabric*, and co-author of *The Art of Classic Quiltmaking*. She is responsible for a myriad of products pertaining to machine quilting, and she has developed batting with Hobbs Bonded Fibers and designed fabric for P&B Textiles.

Carrie has been around quilting all her life—sitting in Harriet's lap as a baby while Harriet sewed, learning her colors with machine embroidery thread and her alphabet on the cams of Harriet's old Viking sewing machine. She didn't have a chance *not* to be involved! Harriet and her mother opened the store when Carrie was four years old, and she spent a part of nearly every day of her life at the store. Carrie's interests in college turned to range management and wildlife biology, but no matter what, she always came home to quilting as a hobby.

In 2006, Harriet decided she wanted to close the store. She was tired after running it for 25 years as well as traveling and teaching at the same time. Carrie couldn't imagine not having the store as a part of her life. So she moved back to Colorado and now runs the store full-time while finishing her master's thesis, "The Physical Properties of Quilting Thread."

Most of all, Carrie is proud to carry on the family legacy of quilting that extends from her great-great-grandmother Phoebie Frazier, to her great-grandmother Harriet Carey, to her grandmother Harriet (Fran) Frazier, to her mom, Harriet. Quilting is all about tradition (no matter how you make a quilt) and about the love of creating something beautiful from fabric and thread with your own hands.

All the quilts in the book were pieced and quilted by Harriet and Carrie. They truly believe that if you are going to teach it, you had better be able to make it!

Resources

SUPPLIES/SOURCE LIST

All notions and supplies referred to in the text are available from

Harriet's Treadle Arts
6390 West 44th Avenue
Wheat Ridge, CO 80033
303-424-2742
www.harriethargrave.com

Information on Harriet's classes, retreats, and conferences can be found on her website.

SEWEZI PORTABLE SEWING TABLES

Quilted Patches
Barbara Huthmacher
P.O. Box 1176
Inyokern, CA 93527
www.seweziusa.com

SEW STEADY TABLES

Dream World Inc.
P.O. Box 89
Bonners Ferry, ID 83805
800-837-3261, ext. 1
www.dreamworld-inc.com

Other books by Harriet Hargrave:

Heirloom Machine Quilting
ISBN 978-1-57120-236-9

Mastering Machine Appliqué
ISBN 978-1-57120-136-2

The following titles are available as downloadable eBooks on www.ctpub.com:

From Fiber to Fabric

Art of Classic Quiltmaking